LIFEBOAT ETHICS

The Moral Dilemmas of World Hunger

LIFEBOAT ETHICS

The Moral Dilemmas of World Hunger

Edited by George R. Lucas, Jr.

and Thomas W. Ogletree

HARPER & ROW, PUBLISHERS

New York, Hagerstown, San Francisco, London

This work was originally published in the Spring 1976 and Summer 1976 issues of *Soundings*.

FIRST EDITION

ISBN: 0-06-065308-6

ISBN: 0-06-065309-4 paper (A Harper Forum Book)

LIBRARY OF CONGRESS CATALOG NUMBER: 76-10002

76 77 78 79 80 81 10 9 8 7 6 5 4 3 2 1

CONTENTS

ACKNOWLEDGMENTS

The bulk of the essays printed in this volume appeared initially as a special issue of *Soundings* (Spring, 1976) which I had the privilege of guest-editing under the title: "Famine and Lifeboat Ethics: Moral Dilemmas in the Formation of Public Policy." I should like to express my gratitude to my colleague Dr. Thomas W. Ogletree, the editor of *Soundings,* and to the editorial committee, for extensive and invaluable assistance in the initial preparation of that issue, and for their permission and assistance in the further preparation of those materials for publication in the present volume. The essays by Donald Shriver and Paul Verghese in this volume appeared initially in the Summer, 1976 issue of *Soundings.* Prof. Shriver's essay, in turn, is based upon a paper read before the January, 1976 meeting of the American Society of Christian Ethics in Washington, D.C.

Both the idea and the need for the present symposium arose in the context of a conference, held in February of 1975, on the topic "Triage in Medicine and Society," which I had the privilege of planning and hosting at the Texas Medical Center's Institute of Religion and Human Development in Houston, Texas. I am grateful to the Director and staff of the Institute, and most especially to my friend and colleague Dr. Kenneth Vaux, for assistance and encouragement, both in that project and in this.

I am indebted to Mr. Lester Brown and the staff of the Worldwatch Institute (Washington, D.C.) for making available to me extensive data, advice, and information of central importance in the preparation of my own essay for this volume. I am also grateful to the editorial staff of Harper & Row Publishers, Inc.—especially Richard Lucas and Clayton Carlson—for their patient and enabling assistance in the realization of this project.

All of the authors represented in this volume contributed their efforts *gratis.* In spite of the wide diversity of opinions expressed, the individual contributors addressed themselves to their respective tasks with promptness and thoroughness, and were most gracious in their relations with one another and with the editors. I should like to take this opportunity to thank them for their courteous efforts in our mutual exploration of so emotionally-trying a subject.

Finally, by mutual agreement of the authors and editors, all author royalties from the publication of this volume are designated for the Hastings Institute for Society, Ethics and the Life Sciences (Hastings-on-Hudson, N.Y.). It is our collective hope that the Fellows of this Institute thereby will be further encouraged to carry on the kind of basic bioethical research so urgently required in the quest for a just and meaningful solution to the difficult problems herein treated, which are of profound and moving concern to us all.

George R. Lucas, Jr.
Evanston, Illinois
March 1, 1976

PREFACE

DANIEL CALLAHAN

S ome problems are difficult because they seem to admit of no solution. Others are difficult because it is almost impossible to reach a consensus on the nature of the problem and thus on what might be done about it. What makes the world food problem so perplexing is that it has been subject to both difficulties. Consider the odd history of the debate itself. During the 1960s, there was a worldwide alarm that starvation might be just around the corner for millions of people. That fear was symbolized in the widely read book by the Paddock brothers, *Famine 1975!* Their argument was stark: the world's population growth was rapidly outstripping its food resources, the Malthusian spectacle of starvation was imminent, and nothing less than a crash program of population control could stave off the inevitable disaster. They also introduced what at the time seemed a shocking proposal. If food aid was to be given at all to needy countries, it should be given only to those which showed a willingness to do something about their own plight and which appeared to have some chance of survival. They used an old term from military medicine,

Dr. Callahan, author of several books and numerous published articles, is the director of the Hastings Institute for Society, Ethics, and the Life Sciences (Hastings-on-Hudson, New York).

"triage," to characterize the nature of their proposal: let the marginally healthy take care of themselves, allow the hopeless cases to die, and center one's efforts on those where aid would make the difference between life and death.

Yet by the early 70s a sharp change had occurred. Spurred by the early success of the Green Revolution, by some scattered hopeful evidence that family planning programs were proving successful, and by the absence of any dramatic instances of mass starvation, the world food crisis was declared over. I was roundly criticized by a reviewer of a book I edited in the early 70s for even including an excerpt from the Paddock & Paddock book, which the reviewer called alarmist and ignorant.

By 1974, however, there was once again a swing of the pendulum. That was the year of the Arab oil boycott and of mass starvation in the Sahel. What the oil boycott made clear was the great dependence of modern agriculture on oil-derived fertilizers. It also made clear, along with other evidence, that the hopes invested in the Green Revolution had been overblown. The Sahel disaster underscored the fragility of life in many parts of the world. As for the success of family planning programs in reducing population growth, the World Population Conference in Bucharest in the summer of 1974 all but exploded that notion. "Famine 1975!" seemed, by the time that year had arrived, to be an exceedingly accurate forecast. Food was once again on the world agenda.

If the rapid shifts in opinion on the world food problem have been bound to create some uncertainty as to whether, and in what way, there is a problem, the plethora of proposed solutions has hardly been less bewildering. Some, at one extreme, do not deny there is a problem. But, they say, it is not a problem of inadequate production but of an inadequate and unjust system of food distribution; the solution is a radical economic and political reform. At the other extreme are those who, while not denying poor distribution, believe that the essence of the problem is a world population growth which continues to outrun the possibility of equivalent food production.

Meanwhile, what ought to be the stance of the United States and, by extension, of the affluent, developed countries of the world? That is the question which lies behind the debate over the "lifeboat ethic." That metaphor, made famous by Garrett Hardin, rests on a number of premises: 1) that the United States cannot possibly solve the world's food problems; 2) that a weakening of our own strength would serve neither our own interests (especially our obligations to future American generations) nor those of the poor countries of the world; 3) that a thoughtless and indiscriminate effort to provide food aid to all claimants could, in the long run, actually make things worse for the countries being helped; and that 4) if the poor countries are to be saved, they will have to save themselves—by effective population control programs, by greater political self-discipline, and by a greater sense of responsibility for their own welfare. Yes, we do live on a rich lifeboat. That is our good fortune. Nothing whatever would be served by our endangering that lifeboat.

I will not try to argue the issues myself here. That is done very ably by the contributors to this volume. I will only record that, like most others, I was initially shocked to see a "lifeboat ethic" proposed with all seriousness and, with it, a revival of the triage argument. At the least, it struck me as a clever exercise in "enlightened" self-interest. The rich have always been known for arguing that their own continued welfare is in the best interests of everyone.

Yet I am not altogether comfortable with a stance of pure condemnation and opposition to a lifeboat ethic. As rich as our nation is, it is not rich enough to solve the world food problem. Some choices must be made: how much aid to provide and to whom and under what circumstances? More than that, even a willingness and an ability to help others is no excuse for irrational action. If it is true, as some advocates of a lifeboat ethic urge, that food aid could actually harm others in the long run, then ordinary morality would suggest the need to at least pause before indiscriminately providing such aid. All actions will have some consequences, and if we have learned anything about contemporary life, it is that good intentions by no means guarantee equally good results. In more areas than one—I am thinking of recent discussions of prison "reform," of "welfare" programs, and urban "renewal"— we have learned how well-intentioned benevolence seems to end by doing more harm than good.

There has also been an additional complication. In the area of both food and other kinds of foreign aid, the United States has, ever since the Second World War, acted out of mixed motives, those of humanitarianism and self-interest. High rhetoric has been combined with a careful calculation about the political pay-off. In recent years, foreign aid appropriations have dropped. For one thing, many of the developing countries (e.g., India) have increasingly come to disdain a dependence upon American aid, which they see both as an instrument of U.S. foreign policy and as a subtle legacy of Western imperialism. For another, burned perhaps by too many failed ventures abroad, the Congress has gradually lost interest in massive aid programs. If nothing else, this trend has revealed how thin the veneer of benevolence and humanitarianism has always been. That is a context which has made the introduction of a lifeboat ethic a good deal more tolerable than might have been the case a decade ago. If "they" don't want our aid anyway, or will take it only if we can be thanked with invective, then why endure the pain of a moral dilemma about whether to give the aid in the first place?

But the moral problem remains. At its deepest level that problem reduces to one of moral obligation. To whom are we obligated and under what circumstances? As a basis of moral obligation, humanitarianism and benevolence are very weak. They depend almost entirely upon the goodwill of those with power or money. It is not that one owes something to those one helps—it is just that one wants, out of charity or kindness, to help them. But, by definition, it is a one-way relationship. As soon as people show themselves ungrateful (and that has been one of the main charges against the recipients of U.S. aid), then the giver feels perfectly justified in stifling the original impulse of kindliness. The old phrase, "the deserving poor," captures perfectly the dynamism—those poor who are, among other things, respectful and grateful. When the humanitarian impulse is combined with a deliberate calculation of self-interest on the part of the giver, then the stage is set for abuse.

Yet it is by no means easy to find a higher ground, at least one that will command the kind of consensus needed to make massive aid available to others. By a "higher ground" I mean a theory of moral obligation toward others which places the emphasis on a duty toward those others, a duty which does not depend upon the vagaries of the way in which, at any given moment, we may feel toward those others. The problem here is an old one. It is not difficult to show that parents have obligations toward their children, or that families have obligations toward each other, or that citizens have obligations toward their nation. In each of those cases, the basis of the obligation is that of mutual need and interdependence. But is it possible to posit duties toward those outside of one's family, community, or national circle? What possible obligations could I have toward total strangers living in another part of the world?

A variety of strategies have surfaced to cope with this question (though the question is not necessarily phrased in the kind of formal moral language I have used). One of the strategies has taken the form of contending that, because of our historical exploitation of the natural and other resources of others, we are therefore obliged to provide compensation. We are rich in great part precisely because we helped to make others poor. Simple justice requires that we right the balance. This is not an altogether easy case to sustain. For one thing, it is often very difficult to find a straight causal relationship between the wealth of our country and specific poverty of another country. It is not enough to invoke a generalized charge of colonialism and imperialism to explain away any and all starvation and malnutrition in developing countries. For another, even if some vague historical correlation can be shown, it is still not clear why the present generation has a specific obligation to make right those wrongs which may have been done by past generations.

Another strategy, summed up in the now-common word "interdependence," would specifically break down the notion that nations are essentially independent of each other. On the contrary, the world is now a large village, with all nations in one respect or another dependent upon each other. If one country or region of the world is in trouble, then the consequences will be felt in other countries and in other parts of the world. The advantage of this strategy is that it does rest upon some simple facts—all nations, for example, now need oil, but all nations do not and cannot produce enough oil to meet their own needs. Yet the disadvantage of this strategy is that many of the poorest countries in the world have nothing to offer the rich countries; they have only poverty and need. Better systems of trade and monetary arrangements will help some of the poorer countries to barter more effectively in a world economy. But it will not help all of them, or even help any of them sufficiently.

"Interdependence" can, and often is, used in a broader sense—that of the "spaceship earth" metaphor. In essence, it is a metaphor which calls attention to the fact that the earth is a limited resource and that, in the long run, the survival of all is at stake. For all the truth of that perception, it is quite general and abstract; the day of reckoning may be so far down the road that it will not serve as an effective goad for those changes necessary to make interdependence a living and efficacious policy in the present historical moment.

In sum, when one looks at those attempts to find a basis for mutual assistance across national boundaries which do not depend simply on the impulse of benevolence, few of them seem to be strong enough to generate the sense of moral obligation which, in principle, the present situation requires.

I called this an "old" argument. By that I meant the tension between our clear obligation on the one hand (family, community, and nation), and our perception of the needs of those outside of that circle on the other. Not surprisingly, it is a dilemma which many would argue can only be solved by the adoption of a religious premise, for only that kind of premise can establish a set of universal obligations. In short, only if one believes that man, say, is "made in the image of God," and if one also believes that the demands of morality go beyond strict notions of duty and obligation—to include also "charity"—can one then posit a morality of sharing and assistance which encompasses all human beings. I personally find this a vexing issue, if only because it is not now the case nor is it ever likely (or desirable) that all human beings will share that ethic. The secular surrogates for that position—some forms of Marxism, for instance—seem so highly dependent upon totalitarian force to achieve the needed sharing that they can only appear morally repugnant.

This is a pessimistic conclusion, at least if one is looking for a way to show that the need of others is in and of itself sufficient to impose obligations on those who could help them. The power of a "lifeboat ethic" is that it builds in very powerful ways upon the duties we have toward our own community. Its profound hazard is that it is an inducement to turn our eyes away from the suffering of others. How we can both serve those we know we must serve while at the same time finding a way to serve those strangers who are in need may well be one of the great moral dramas of our time.

POLITICAL AND ECONOMIC DIMENSIONS OF HUNGER: Strategies to Combat Famine in the 1970's

GEORGE R. LUCAS, Jr.

T HE DIRECTOR of a major church-sponsored disaster relief
agency recently characterized the present international
crisis of hunger and malnutrition as presenting a choice among
three alternative strategies: lifeboat ethics, triage, and unqualified assistance. This extreme oversimplification is
characteristic of the current emotionally charged confusion
which has enveloped a significant portion of the international
community in the wake of sudden and acute shortages of vital
commodities.

This confusion is understandably a reflection of the largely
unanticipated onslaught of the shortages themselves. In 1972,
for example, the world community witnessed India, its graneries
overflowing from the first fruits of its "green revolution," providing several million tons of grain to an estimated ten million
Bengali refugees, and later providing similar assistance to the
newly created nation of Bangladesh. This was accomplished by a
large and overpopulated nation which had itself until very recently been among the world's leading importers of food.

Mr. Lucas is a doctoral student in philosophy of religion and ethics at
Northwestern University, and Research Associate at the Peace Institute,
Garrett-Evangelical Seminary (Evanston, Ill.). He has edited one volume of a
monograph series on medical ethics, *Triage in Medicine and Society* (Houston:
Institute of Religion, 1975), and has written articles on social ethics, public
policy, and world affairs.

1

For the most part international food prices and supplies at this time were fluctuating only modestly in response to inflation. Thousands of acres of fertile cropland were being held idle in the United States, and an "energy crisis" for most persons was only a vague and futuristic nightmare. Small wonder that a distinguished economist at Massachusetts Institute of Technology could state at that time:

> . . . the prospects of a world famine crisis in the foreseeable short-run period, such as the next three decades, are not compelling—although large pockets of undernourished areas, reflecting low incomes rather than world scarcity of food, cannot unfortunately be ruled out . . . indeed, the notion of a world famine, arising from food scarcity and over-whelming us by 2000 A.D., seems to me altogether fanciful.[1]

A scant two years later, however, India suffered the second consecutive failure of her annual monsoons, while a record drought continued in the African Sahel. These factors, combined with dramatic worldwide price increases and scarcities of fertilizer and fossil fuels, set in motion a self-reinforcing cycle of inflated prices and widespread shortages of food and other essential commodities. This in turn sent the international economy into a tailspin of recession, and brought on a virtual worldwide panic. The revised forecasts of stunned economists and agronomists indicated, for the near future at least, the chilling spectre of economic collapse, political chaos, and world famine looming dangerously near. These sudden developments provided decisive vindication for those who had warned of the finiteness and overstress of both the global ecosystem and the international economy,[2] and refuted the majority of the world's leaders and peoples, who had clung to the naively-optimistic hope that the "Mad Hatter's teaparty" of industrial, agricultural, and demographic growth and consumption could continue indefinitely.

Against this background of frustration and fear, harsh and tough-minded proposals for selective allocation and distribution of the world's important resources—that is, proposals advocating triage and lifeboat ethics— began to emerge (or, in some cases, to re-emerge) in 1974.[3]. Proponents of these measures reasoned that past "give-away" programs had failed to alleviate hunger and its root causes, and that an insufficiency of important commodities existed for distribution among an incessantly burgeoning world population. Hard choices therefore had to be faced concerning who was the most "worthy" among potential recipients to receive the available aid. In the extreme such proposals argued that grants of food and other assistance should be strictly conditional upon successful attempts by prospective recipients to alleviate the root causes of hunger and poverty, principally identified as uncontrolled population growth.[4]

Predictably, critical reaction to such proposals has been overwhelmingly negative. A great many of these negative responses—formulated by otherwise capable, knowledgeable, and intelligent persons—have, however, exhibited as much unrestrained emotionalism as reasoned consideration of the critical issues at hand. This emotionalism in itself gives some indication both of the confusion and fear generated by the present aura of crisis and of the severity of the triage and lifeboat ethics proposals themselves.

Allocating food, for example, on a strict *quid pro quo* basis—implying that those peoples and nations who cannot (or will not) control their population growth and put their political houses in order may be left to starve—does seem on the surface to violate basic moral and humanitarian principles in a fundamental way. Whether the enactment of selective allocation policies *would* in fact violate these principles is, however, a highly debatable point. Indeed, the debate on this issue is central to the substance of the present collection of essays.

In addition the precise relationships and similarities between the "triage" and "lifeboat ethics" strategies are far from clear. Does either of these descriptive metaphors suggest a more acceptable or helpful strategy for dealing with scarcities than the other—or, as critics have contended, are both metaphors finally and equally bankrupt in moral perspective?

Finally, attempts to classify triage and lifeboat ethics as two of three alternatives for dealing with global famine (the third being unqualified food assistance), are inaccurate and highly misleading. There exist, in fact, a plethora of strategies and proposals for combating the worldwide phenomenon of hunger and malnutrition which admit to none of these extremes, and which challenge the fundamental premises both of unrestricted and of highly restricted forms of assistance.

Debate on the merits of selective allocation *vis à vis* other alternatives, together with evaluations of the social, political, and moral consequences of each, form the content of the essays which follow. As preparation for the debate to come, I shall attempt in the remainder of the present essay to outline and describe the major alternative proposals for combating hunger and world famine. For simplicity I shall group these various strategies under three broad categories.

I. *Donative schemes* embrace for the most part a principle of "unqualified assistance." These include programs of outright food grants (or alternatively, cash grants or long-term, low interest loans to purchase food) to be distributed to those most severely afflicted by malnutrition. This category also includes the spot "disaster relief" programs to combat hunger and disease following in the wake of natural catastrophes or war.

II. *Developmental or self-help schemes* focus on the "supply—demand" equation among the most severely afflicted populations or geographical regions, attempting more frequently to aid developing countries in augmenting their supply of food, and less frequently to aid in reducing the pressure of excessive demand through voluntary programs of population control.

III. *Selective allocation strategies* are principally represented by the triage and lifeboat ethics proposals, which seek to control hunger by alternately giving and withholding aid based upon the willingness of recipients to grant concessions in return, such as agreeing to a strict regulation of population growth.

I. DONATIVE SCHEMES

Until comparatively recent times, the principal strategy to combat widespread hunger and malnutrition involved unconditional, short-term grants of food, or of cash funds to purchase food on the world market. This assistance commonly followed in the wake of severe famines in specific geographical areas (such as those in India in 1943 and again in 1964), or was provided to the survivors either of natural catastrophes (principally earthquakes, typhoons, and floods) or of war (such as the Biafran victims during the 1969–70 Nigerian civil war, or the refugees from the Bengali war for independence mentioned earlier). This aid focused on the "target groups" suffering the most severe effects of undernourishment: young children, pregnant women, nursing mothers, and the elderly. The primary voluntary organizations engaged in this relief work—e.g., CARE and OXFAM, together with church-sponsored agencies such as Church World Service, the Catholic Relief Agencies, and the United Methodist Committee on Relief—held it an unquestionable assumption that such programs represented the only appropriate and humane response to the tragedy of hunger-induced suffering.

To a lesser extent national governments participated as well in unconditional food aid programs. The United States, for example, under Title II of Public Law 480 distributed national food surpluses on a limited grant basis to other governments, to some of the private organizations named above, and occasionally to the only truly international program currently in existence, the United Nations World Food Programme. Government-sponsored programs such as "Food for Peace," where they exist at all, exist primarily for the benefit of the donor government, providing a convenient channel for disbursing excess food resources without abnormal depressive effects on domestic food prices. In addition government programs frequently reserve the lion's share of available food surpluses for distribution in accordance with political objectives in the conduct of their foreign policy (e.g., the distribution of U. S. surpluses under Title I of P. L. 480).[5] For this reason existing government food programs are more appropriately grouped under the rubric of selective allocation (a subject to which we shall presently return).

Stuart Hinds in the present collection mentions the pioneering efforts of Lord Boyd-Orr, founder of the U. N. Food and Agricultural Organization, to establish a world food board in 1948. The proposal has been revived in this decade in a variety of forms, including a proposal by Lester Brown for a U. N. Disaster Relief Force and the proposal by A. H. Boerma of the F.A.O. for a system of internationally-coordinated national food-reserve policies.[6] (Joseph Fletcher's call for a World Food Bank is differentiated from the foregoing proposals in part by his stipulation that this organization permit *no* unconditional grants of food assistance.) At the 1974 World Food Conference in Rome, representatives of the Oil Producing and Exporting Countries (OPEC) augmented the discussion of an international food reserve by laudably calling for the creation of an Agricultural Development Fund. This fund would facilitate the reinvestment of surplus OPEC capital in agricultural development projects benefiting impoverished countries; it illustrates the emerging trend for such proposals in the current decade.

Donative agencies function primarily to provide short-term disaster relief, seeking to avert the tragic effects of impending famine through the direct and immediate provision of food supplies. Critics of these policies have charged, however, that such relief treats only the symptoms and not the root causes of hunger. Instead of providing short-term, terminal relief, such policies frequently create situations of permanent dependency on surplus food supplies.

In response to such criticisms voluntary and church-sponsored relief agencies have begun in recent years to take fresh stock of the oft-quoted Chinese proverb: "Give me a fish and I eat today; teach me to fish and I eat for a lifetime." Such agencies have also been forced to re-examine past policies in light of the increasing requests from third-world leaders for aid in the attainment of a measure of self-sufficiency for their countries as a necessary prerequisite to the achievement of full liberation and human dignity. The present trend, illustrated by the OPEC proposal in Rome, thus has shifted from donations to development.

II. DEVELOPMENT SCHEMES: PROBLEMS, PROSPECTS AND CONSEQUENCES

During recent years nearly every agency engaged in the war against famine and poverty has focused on increasing the self-sufficiency and productivity of indigenous agriculture and industry in afflicted countries. The wide prevalence and use of the designations "developing" and "developed" to distinguish the relative economic status and progressiveness of nations reveals the overwhelming preoccupation with this strategy, as does the now-familiar distinction between affluent nations and "third world"—even "fourth world"—countries.[7]

A wide variety of development-oriented projects has been attempted. Government-sponsored projects include the Soviet-sponsored Aswan Dam in Egypt, which sought to harness the Nile both to provide hydroelectric power for increased industrialization and to enable increased irrigation of arid but potentially fertile farmland. CARE has for many years provided, along with food relief, basic farming tools and primary-school education materials for children. The United Methodist Committee on Relief (UMCOR) recently has shifted its focus from providing foodstuffs to purchasing and marketing fertilizers to small farmers on a sliding-scale financial basis. The Lilly foundation has sponsored pilot irrigation projects in several West African countries, while the Ford and Rockefeller foundations joined forces in the 1960's to underwrite the basic genetic research of Nobel-laureate Norman Borlaug and others, thus aiding the discovery of the new "miracle strains" of wheat and rice which heralded the "Green Revolution."

These are but a small sample of the myriad number of development and self-help projects which have been sponsored, are currently in operation, or recently have been proposed. All such projects, however, hold one strategy in common: they focus on the basic supply-demand equation, seeking either to *augment* the world's food supply through improved agricultural methods or other technological innovations, or to *reduce* the overall world food demand through increased efficiency and the elimination of waste and needless consumption, and through a variety of programs stressing control of population growth.

1. *Increasing Food Supplies*

In the final analysis, observes agricultural expert Lester Brown, there are only two ways to increase the overall quantity of the world harvest: either by bringing more land under cultivation, or by increasing the yield per acre. That observation in turn reveals the ultimate dependency of the agricultural enterprise on four variables: land, water, energy, and fertilizer. The various development programs now in operation reduce finally to an emphasis upon one or more of these critical variables.[8]

Land

The image of the early American frontiersman clearing his land, farming, and subsequently moving on to repeat the process elsewhere is a wholly familiar one. From the beginnings of agriculture until about 1950, according to Brown and Erik Eckholm, this expansion of cultivated area was the major method for increasing crop yields. Now, however, with more than eleven percent of the earth's total land surface under cultivation, there are few places left to plow. Those few areas which may yet possess new agricultural potential will offer formidable obstacles to profitable farming due to scarce or poor-quality topsoil, lack of fresh water, inhospitable climates, and so forth.

Brown and Eckholm comment that their perspective is in sharp contrast to estimates which optimistically emphasize the sizeable areas of land still remaining to be cultivated. They argue that the more optimistic estimates are of little value since they fail to stress *at what cost* additional land may be made productive, and do not reveal the food-price levels at which the resultant farming could be made profitable.[9]

Moreover, while new land may be brought under cultivation in the future through monumental efforts and extreme expenditures, hundreds of thousands of acres of fertile cropland are yearly being lost elsewhere around the globe. Areas denuded of natural cover through overgrazing of grasslands or through excessive fuel and industrial demands upon forests quickly lose their precious topsoil—thousands of years in the making—to the eroding influences of wind and water. Even more inexcusably, developed countries thoughtlessly sacrifice thousands of acres of farmland annually to urban growth. Estimates of the amount of cropland lost to airports, housing developments, shopping centers and urban recreation areas are upwards of half a million acres annually. This loss occurs with little regard for the long-term consequences.[10]

Current development programs have in part focused upon bringing new land under cultivation (through irrigation projects, for example). In the future these programs may give increased emphasis to emulating America's successful recovery of farmland during the Great Plains "dust bowl" era in the 1930's, by likewise reclaiming once-fertile land that has been lost to agriculture through erosion (e.g., the recent, highly-expensive "greenhousing" enclosure of semi-desert lands in the Sahel). Such projects are bound to be costly, however, both technologically and financially—and the Brown-Eckholm analysis warns against over-optimistic expectations of such efforts in the future.

The other alternative for development schemes concerned with land use is to bring about an increase in the yield per acre of land already under cultivation. Since about 1950 such "intensification of cultivation" has accounted for the lion's share of the annual increase in world agricultural output by utilizing improved seeds and more efficient farming techniques, such as multiple cropping. Where climate and other conditions are favorable, raising the output per acre depends substantially on the availability of the three remaining variables: water, energy, and fertilizer.

Water

Brown and Eckholm observe that, despite the difficulties just mentioned in expanding the quantity of arable land, "the principal constraint on efforts to expand world food supplies during the final years of this century may well be water rather than land." This is in part due to the fact that the majority of rivers, streams, and other sources of fresh water which are capable of being dammed or otherwise harnessed for irrigation already have been developed. In the future, say these experts, efforts to increase the supply of fresh water will have to rely increasingly upon novel techniques, such as desalinization of seawater, manipulation of rainfall (climatology), or the diversion of rivers. Unfortunately, development schemes thus far proposed or attempted which utilize these techniques either have proved excessively expensive or have manifested unanticipated and undesirable ecological side-effects.[11]

Finally, massive irrigation can itself cause untoward side effects, principally by raising the underground water table to within a few feet or even inches of the surface. Resultant water-logging inhibits the growth of plant roots. More significantly, the evaporation of water from the soil at this level vastly increases the salt and mineral deposits in the topsoil, eventually forcing the abandonment of the land (as recently occurred in Pakistan). Awesome, long-range social consequences of this latter kind are evident in the historical record and are exemplified by the successive decline of the Tigris-Euphrates valley—and comparatively more recently, western North Africa—from fertile and densely-populated agricultural centers in the ancient world to sparsely-populated, barren wasteland today.

As a result, future development projects stressing the expansion of agriculture to meet the food demands of a growing world population must develop a new system of accounting: the per-capita "water costs" of various new techniques and of old habits must be included in the equations of agricultural expansion.

A person subsisting on a vegetarian diet of 2.5 pounds of bread a day is indirectly utilizing 300 gallons of water daily. Production of food for an affluent diet of two pounds of vegetable matter and one pound of beef and animal fat a day, by contrast, requires a total of about 2,500 gallons of water daily. The "water cost" of a pound of beef—which includes that used to produce feed as well as that drunk by the animal—is about twenty-five times that of a pound of bread . . .[12]

Energy

The energy factor influences the agricultural enterprise at the most fundamental level. Basically, the energy yield of the crop produced (measured in calories) must equal or surpass the energy of human muscle expended by the farm family and other workers, or they will not survive. At the dawn of human agriculture, this factor bound virtually all non-nomadic or non-hunting peoples to the soil.

The "energy efficiency"—the ratio of food calories produced to those expended in the production—vastly improved with the harnessing of draft animals to aid in the performance of agricultural labor, even after accounting for the additional food consumed by the animals. The size of this "energy efficiency ratio" dictates the percentage of a population which can be freed from agriculture for other pursuits, in turn permitting the development of advanced civilizations and cultures.

The size of the energy efficiency ratio apparently took a "great leap forward" in the twentieth century with the development of farm implements powered by fossil fuels. The quantity of fuel consumed seemed to enter the energy factor only modestly and indirectly. The machinery itself permitted a reduction in the use of animals (which must be fed in the winter as well as grazed in the summer), yet simultaneously permitted a vast magnification in the labor and production possibilities of a farm family. It therefore appeared as though a genuine and massive breakthrough had been achieved. These developments have made possible the remarkable situation in the United States whereby some five percent of the population directly engaged in agriculture are able to feed an entire nation and to export considerable quantities of food as well.

Growing realization of the finiteness of fossil fuel supplies, coupled with escalating prices and increasing scarcities, has revealed the *illusion* of the apparently high energy efficiency ratio in modern agriculture, and has forced a re-assessment of the total situation with devastating conclusions. "If energy accounting . . . is used to evaluate the efficiency of food production systems," argue Brown and Eckholm, "a surprising fact emerges. The books are not balancing for the more advanced agricultural systems, which are running up an energy deficit." In the U. S., for example, ". . . by 1970 nearly nine calories were being consumed by the system for every calorie contained in the food produced." Furthermore, Brown and Eckholm maintain that the greatest inefficiency in the modern system occurs not on the farm itself, but in the processing, transportation, and distribution of the food.[13]

These observations carry momentous implications for future development projects. On the basis of the "illusion of the high energy efficiency ratio" in modern agriculture, government and privately-sponsored development programs in the fifties and sixties sought to persuade third-world farmers to "modernize" (meaning "mechanize"). The consequent mechanization of a sizeable portion of third-world agriculture (ranging from a few diesel irrigation pumps and a small tractor on modest farms to extensive mechanization of larger, commercially-owned tracts) has made that enterprise overly dependent upon supplies of fossil fuels. These measures also encouraged the consolidation of land holdings from small family tracts to larger, mechanized farm "businesses," displacing the poorer families from their land and throwing potentially-useful laborers into the ranks of the unemployed. This result in turn further exacerbated the maldistribution of income, consequently increasing poverty and malnutrition.[14]

The OPEC oil embargo in 1973–74 revealed the folly of these policies and trends. The high cost and virtual unavailability of fossil fuels combined with poor weather to bring the agricultural enterprise in the developing countries to its knees. Farmers in affluent countries were for the most part still able to pay the higher prices and to obtain vital supplies of fuel, passing the increased costs along to the consumers—who for the most part were likewise able to pay. Farmers and consumers in developing countries were in no position to compete.

These observations indicate that henceforth development and self-help agricultural schemes will ignore the energy efficiency ratio in agriculture at their peril. Far more attention must be paid to balancing total energy accounts in the food production process. In the future an optimal balance must be struck between mechanization and the use of local laborers and draft animals, thereby minimizing over-dependence upon any but indigenous sources of production energy. In human terms this balance means not only decreased strain on the environment and on energy resources, but also full employment, more equitable income distribution, reduction of poverty, and consequently, an improvement in nutrition.

Fertilizer

This final factor enters the picture both as an independent commodity, presently experiencing its own problems of high prices and scarcity, and as a consequence of the energy problem just described. As Brown points out, the manufacture of nitrogen fertilizer requires large amounts of natural gas as a raw material, is energy-intensive in its production, and requires further energy for transportation and application to the farmland.

Scarcities of fertilizer in recent years were in part attributable to the lack of new production facilities. These facilities are now being constructed in many parts of the world, leading Alan Berg of the World Bank to conclude optimistically that in the near future there will be plenty of fertilizer for everybody.[15] Indeed, if the vast quantities of natural gas presently wasted at wellheads in the Middle East were utilized in production, this prediction could well be realized for the immediate future, although the *cost* of such fertilizers would still be too high for poorer farmers to afford.

The current problem to be faced in this regard is that of priority use and distribution of fertilizer—a problem underscored by the embargo imposed on fertilizer exports by affluent countries during the height of recent scarcities. Fertilizer use follows a "law of diminishing returns." Initial applications can bring a remarkable increase in crop yields. After a certain point, however (between 80 and 120 pounds of nitrogen fertilizer per acre of corn, for example[16]), the ratio of increased yields (measured in pounds) per pound of fertilizer applied decreases rapidly to unity. In most developed countries the optimal point on the "fertilizer response curve" has now been surpassed. Given the high cost and scarcity of fertilizer, massive new applications in such countries very literally represent money and energy down the drain.

By contrast those same new applications of fertilizer, were

they made available to farmers in developing countries, would bring about dramatic increases in crop yields on land which heretofore has received little or no fertilizer. Food production would thus be increased precisely in the areas of greatest need at a minimal comparative expenditure of money and energy. Precisely for this reason the fertilizer embargo by developed countries was an act of monumental stupidity: these countries now are pressured to devise far more costly methods of dealing with drastic crop failures in developing countries—costs and failures which could have been averted in part by a wise and far-sighted priority allocation of fertilizers.

Also for these reasons third-world fertilizer distribution programs (such as that recently inaugurated by UMCOR) make sense—for the moment at least. But the "law of diminishing returns" regarding fertilizer application places limits even on this form of expanding agricultural productivity. Coupled with the problems encountered regarding the preceding agricultural variables, the fertilizer problem ultimately underscores the very legitimate warnings of "selective allocation" advocates that the present development emphasis on endlessly increasing food supplies must finally give way to more effective measures for stabilizing or reducing food demands.

Whatever Happened to the Green Revolution?

At this point in the discussion those in favor of supply-development schemes may be wondering what happened to the most heralded of all such programs: *viz.*, the distribution of new high-yield seed varieties intended to promote a "Green Revolution." The answer to that question is complex, but it is provided in part by commenting that this "revolution" is neither accomplished nor totally defeated. It has, however, run into some severe and largely-unanticipated obstacles. That the "Green Revolution" was at least partially successful is illustrated by the spectacle of brief Indian grain reserves which I cited at the outset.

In the 1960's when Norman Borlaug and others engaged in the genetic research for new high-yield varieties of wheat and rice, fertilizer and energy shortages were only dimly-perceived difficulties on the far horizon. The obstacles to high crop yields were for the most part disease, insects and other pests, oversensitivity of some crops to climate fluctuations (such as the length of

the day or of the growing season), and poor-to-moderate responses of important staple crops to fertilizer application.
Borlaug's "miracle wheat" was in response remarkably disease-
resistant, possessed an insensitive "biological clock" (enabling its
use in a variety of different locales and climatic situations), and
was highly responsive to large applications of fertilizer. Its use in
place of traditional varieties greatly increased crop yields per
acre, permitting India over a seven-year period to achieve an
historically unparalleled expansion in its food production.[17]

Unfortunately the time-tarnished and much-abused adage,
"You don't get something for nothing," proved altogether true
in this case. Brown observes that the genetic potentials of miracle
wheats and rices can be realized only with heavy applications of
fertilizer. In addition the benefits of the new seeds tend to be
more fully realized on larger, mechanized farms, further
encouraging that unfortunate trend. The fertilizer scarcities
and energy shortages of the 1970's—the latter preventing the
operation of irrigation pumps and farm machinery—have
therefore dealt a devastating blow to the progress of the
"Revolution."

Finally, the initial success of the new cereal breeds masked to
some extent the fact that the chief problem encountered in
developing countries is *protein* malnutrition. The fascination
with high-yield cereals in fact may have contributed to a slight
decline in the production of less-dramatic high protein crops,
such as beans, peas, and soybeans—all of which (as nitrogen-
fixing legumes) *provide* soil nutrients rather than requiring ex-
ternal applications of fertilizer. The chief failure of the "Green
Revolution," according to Brown and Eckholm, may be the
failure of scientists to increase dramatically the per acre yield of
soy beans.[18]

It may be questioned whether new technologies in agriculture
represent a "fifth independent variable" in the food equation.
The results of the "Green Revolution" suggest that in the final
analysis they do not. Agricultural technologies—as do all other
supply-development schemes—finally depend strictly upon the
"four agricultural variables" (land, water, energy, and fertilizer)
which Brown and Eckholm have correctly identified. The
"Revolution" may have staved off even greater disaster and
suffering for the present, but clearly this represents only "borrowed time." The disappointing results of this most heralded

development strategy force us back once again toward the uncomfortable half of the crucial equation—a reduction in food demand.

Other Strategies for Food Supply Development

Some time ago Alan Berg analyzed then-current trends and offered proposals for the role of private enterprise and multinational corporations in the fight against hunger.[19] Given the present controversy surrounding the nature and place of "multinationals" in global society—and allowing for the intervening variables of energy shortages and economic recession—several of his proposals still seem appropriate today. These include the sharing of corporate distribution facilities to market low-cost foods under government programs, marshalling the skills of private industry (specifically advertising) to devise educational programs that create greater nutrition awareness, making available industrial research capabilities and facilities in host countries for government programs, working with local governments to produce processed foods for distribution in public institutional feeding programs, and contracting with local governments to meet a predetermined nutritional objective (e.g., designing new products to meet certain nutritional and consumer specifications and distributing such products effectively to the areas of greatest need).

Many multinational corporations—particularly the large food conglomerates, such as Kraft, Coca-Cola, Nestle, and General Foods—have indeed engaged in these and other similar projects. They have been stimulated to do so by a variety of motivations, such as a desire for improved relations with local or home governments or the general public, profit, new market competition, and a genuine sense of social good and public service. Much potential yet remains to be explored in this area, though Brown, Eckholm, and others have expressed approval and hope at the limited successes of such projects as the third-world marketing of soy-meat substitutes and protein-enriched soft drinks.

In a separate vein Elizabeth Mann Borgese writes with enthusiasm about the coming of the "Blue Revolution,"[20] as human beings make the transition from hunters and foragers to ocean farmers, "domesticating" important marine animal and plant life, and vastly increasing yields. The potential for profitable fish farming has been around for a long time. The Chinese, for example, developed complex carp-farming techniques thousands of years ago. In the U. S. today the limited farming of fresh-water catfish and trout, and of saltwater shellfish, has met with considerable success. Recently, reports Borgese, scientists at the Woods Hole Oceanographic Institution developed a remarkable method of fish farming, based upon the Chinese ecological fish-culture model. The system utilizes human sewage from a nearby treatment plant as fertilizer for algae, and ultimately produces oysters, fish, edible seaweeds, and fresh water!

In contrast, however, the present status of ocean fisheries appears grim. Having increased over the years by several million tons annually, the world fish catch has finally begun to stabilize—and even to decline. Lester Brown and others speculate that the worldwide catch of edible fish is now at or beyond the maximum sustainable level (that is, to increase the catch further will deplete the stocks faster than the fish can reproduce, as occurred with the Peruvian anchovie fisheries in the early seventies). As for the prospects of fish farming, Brown dismisses immediate hopes for a miracle, arguing that extensive yields from fish farming await further advances in technology and extensive capital investment in fish farming facilities.

In the final analysis the most hopeful development strategies are those which aim at increasing overall efficiency and reducing waste in the entire agricultural system. Brown and Eckholm imply that this is best achieved by replacing current emphases on mechanization and land consolidation with land reforms and renewed emphasis on the small private farm. The latter—utilizing an optimal balance of human, animal, and machine labor to grow a proper balance of fertilizer-dependent, high-yield cereals and nutrient-restoring, high protein legumes—would encourage a full-employment economy, helping to combat poverty and ensuring an adequate share in the food supply. In addition this mode of farming alone is able to maximize the ratio of total food output per unit of human, animal, and fossil energy expended. Examples of nations where such policies have succeeded dramatically include Taiwan, Japan, and the Peoples' Republic of China.

2. *Decreasing Food Demand*

With supply-development strategies for the most part beset on all sides by as many problems as promises, increasing attention has been paid to the more delicate and uncomfortable problem of reducing food demand. There is far less to report in this regard, because far less has been accomplished. Efforts toward increasing food supplies make everyone happy: they seem to imply that we can "let everyone eat cake" merely by devising better and better methods to bake more and more cakes. The preceding survey provides grounds for doubting that hypothesis.

Talk of reducing demand, however, makes everyone uncomfortable. In contrast to the supply problem, there are only a few ways to "reduce the demand," virtually all of which challenge someone's moral beliefs, aspirations, hopes, dreams, or long-established habits.

There are to my knowledge only two non-violent strategies to reduce food demand: halting population growth (with a goal of stablizing or even reducing the total population) and ending waste, profligacy, and overconsumption.

Population Control

Few reasonable persons any longer doubt the *need* for some form of population control. Differences and conflicts arise for the most part over *which* methods and *whose* strategies will be adopted to gain the necessary control. The available options ultimately boil down either to *reducing* the birth rate (until the birth-to-death ratio becomes less than one), or allowing the death rate to *increase* until the same effect is achieved. Commenting on the latter approach to the problem, Brown and Eckholm maintain that "reliance on rising death rates to alleviate food scarcity is neither morally nor, in the long run, politically acceptable."[21] Other observers (notably Paul Ehrlich and Garrett Hardin) have argued persuasively, however, that if birth rates are not reduced *immediately, by whatever persuasive or coercive means necessary*, then the laws of natural ecology will step in most assuredly to do the job at the other end of the scale.[22]

The emphasis of population control programs since World War II has been largely persuasive, seeking voluntary reduction of birth rates through educational programs, gift and cash incentives, and low-cost or free distribution of condoms, oral contraceptives, intrauterine devices (IUD's), and most recently, programs of free vasectomies for men. With limited exceptions the results have been dismal. In India, for example, where a variety of such measures have been tried since 1952, only about eight percent of the women, and far fewer men, have availed themselves of birth control devices.[23] (The Japanese government, however, has sponsored a low-cost program of "abortion on demand" during the past two decades which, evaluated *strictly* from the standpoint of population control, has been relatively successful.)

Massive failures in past birth control programs have been explained in part by a conflict with religious and social customs, as well as a fear in the third world of traditionally-high mortality rates (especially *infant* mortality rates). The former reasons present something of an impasse, which possibly could be overcome by more effective programs of re-education, or by seeking out and offering only those forms of birth control that do *not* seem to violate customs and beliefs (whenever such methods can be discovered).

The latter observation on high mortality rates, however, has given rise to the most widely prevalent explanation—and resultant paradigm—for the birth-population question: the "demographic transition theory." A nutritional version of this theory was presented before the World Health Organization in the early 1950's by Brazilian Josue de Castro; in a variety of forms the theory is currently maintained by such distinguished authorities as Roger Revelle and Lester R. Brown.

> An assured food supply plays an important role in reducing birth rates. When malnutrition is widespread, even common childhood diseases are often fatal. *The relationship between nutrition and human fertility is summed up in the observation that good nutrition is the best contraceptive.*[24]

The assumptions here are as follows: (1) A certain number of living children at the end of the normal child-rearing period is a desirable thing, in order to assist in agricultural chores, provide for security in old age, fulfill longstanding expectations of cultural and religious traditions, and for the pure pride and satisfaction of having a family. (2) High mortality rates among infants and children (caused by malnutrition, disease, and other side-effects of poverty) historically have necessitated high fertility rates to accomplish these goals. Families cannot be expected to reduce birth rates voluntarily without suitable guarantees that the fewer number of children produced all can survive to adulthood. (3) Conversely, affluent peoples, possessing such security, can be observed to have reduced fertility rates voluntarily. (4)

Thus, income redistribution and resource sharing, enabling all persons to cross a yet-to-be-determined "socio-economic threshold" are the major answer to population control. In this form the demographic transition theory thus provides the present motivation for increasing all forms of foreign aid to developing and impoverished countries.

The widespread acceptance and crucially-important implications of the demographic transition theory warrant a brief digression at this point. Both Joseph Fletcher and Garrett Hardin attack that theory in these pages, particularly the authenticity of the third proposition. Hardin prefers an explanation of population based upon what he terms "Gregg's Law." While he obviously accepts the theory, Lester Brown nevertheless is cognizant of a number of nations which have proved exceptions to the theory, noticeably reducing their birth rates and population growth *without* a large prior increase in total GNP or per capita income.[25]

In my opinion the legitimacy of emphasizing proposals to *increase* food supplies over those to *decrease* food demands depends upon the veridicality of this theory. If the theory is fundamentally correct, then proposals advocating increased food supplies, massive income redistribution, and diversion of significant percentages of the affluent countries' GNP's toward development projects are clearly justified (a conclusion that would be fully congruent with the consensus of most contemporary liberation philosophies). It would then be reasonable to predict success for those strategies in attaining the twin goals of a stabilized world population and a decent basic standard of living for all the world's peoples. If the theory is *false*, however, we are forced to take full and serious appraisal of the harsh and presently unpopular theories advanced under the rubric of "selective allocation."

In this regard the contention by Brown and Eckholm that "the historical record indicates that human fertility does not usually decline unless certain basic social needs are satisfied,"[26] simply will not hold up in the cold light of day. The "historical record" is, rather, highly ambiguous at this point. It may be even more correct to assert that in fact *fertility* rates (which are the number of viable *pregnancies* per unit population) never have varied to any *significant* degree anywhere at any time in recorded history, *regardless* of nutritional or socio-economic levels. The variations have occurred rather in the *mortality rates* (as Dr. Hinds suggests in his essay), both in response to the above factors and more recently in response to technological changes and innovations.

This deceptively simple restatement places the population problem in far clearer and more awesome perspective. Advocates of selective allocation well may have history on *their* side with the pessimistic anticipation that mortality rates indeed will fluctuate once again in order to "rebalance" the present global situation. Attempting to avert that impending disaster through a reduction in human fertility, however—quite in contrast to the statements by advocates of the demographic transition theory—commits us to an enterprise *never before attempted* in human history, irrespective of income and food supplies. Yet it is this enterprise which may offer the only humane solution to famine and poverty.

Excessive Consumption

Alan Berg comments that

> . . . (the) uncertainties that pervade the population field have been compounded by the aggressive attitudes of richer countries that want poorer countries to adopt population programs. Friction has led to politicization of the issue—sometimes with racial overtones—that has hindered acceptance of population policies.[27]

Suspicion by third-world representatives is in part well founded (though it should not hinder developing countries from pursuing population control in their own interest). There is something inherently fraudulent about affluent peoples engaging in smug condemnation of the world's poor while seated at an overflowing supper table.

As is frequently pointed out, the average North American consumes roughly five times as much grain as the average Indian or Bengali (much of this indirectly in the form of meat, milk, and eggs), not to mention a disproportionately large share of the world's other resources, including energy. Less frequently stressed is the obvious and logical conclusion that, if this is true, then even a *modest* growth of population in North America puts as much or more strain on the global ecosystem as does a much larger population growth in most developing countries. Indeed far more helpful than current population statistics would be a system of "weighted" population growth figures, adjusted for the average per capita consumption of the existing population in each country or region being analyzed. Such revised "weighted population growth" statistics would clearly show the U. S. and other developed, affluent countries equal to or surpassing the population growth of such traditional "culprits" as India and Mexico.

Despite expressed fears to the contrary, elimination of over-consumption does not necessarily imply an unacceptable reduction in the standard of living. Figures show that West Germany and Japan, for example, consume only about twice the per capita amount of food resources of the poorest countries.[28] Both of these nations, but particularly West Germany, are considered to be relatively affluent, developed, and progressive with a majority of citizens enjoying a more-than-adequate standard of living. The living habits of the people in such nations are worth investigating, for they contradict the notion that modest reductions in our standard of living come at the expense of comfort and happiness.[29] Such countries may point the way for many North Americans as we awake from our post-war, post-Depression fears of thirty years standing to the previously unthinkable notion that a "Law of Diminishing Returns" applies to consumerism as well as to fertilizer application. Indeed, a recent analysis of the world economy by London's *Financial Times* analyst Paul Lewis[30] provides grounds for the hope that Americans and others are indeed re-awakening to the age-old axiom that, beyond a certain level, the quality of life is not necessarily enhanced merely by increasing the quantity of goods produced, possessed, or consumed.

One needless pattern of overconsumption severely criticized of late is the North American love affair with grain-fed or "heavy" beef. It is a love affair with tragic consequences that we could well afford to end. Recent medical studies show that Americans purchase the added flavor and texture of heavy beef at severe long-range peril to their health; the high fat content of such meat (as much as 50 percent in the choicest cuts) has been linked with coronary diseases and several forms of digestive-tract cancer. In addition the more nutritious, healthful and less-expensive forms of grass-fed "light beef" (which were the *only* varieties of beef extensively available prior to the mid-1950's) utilize in their production vegetable substances which are of no direct nutritional value to humans. Greater dependence on these traditional, range-fed varieties of animal protein, in addition to bringing better health and greater savings for the consumer, would release hundreds of thousands of acres of fertile cropland—currently used to grow fertilizer-intensive feed corn—for the increased farming of wheat and soybeans, thereby augmenting the world supply of these precious commodities as well.

Other areas of waste and excessive consumption in affluent countries—such as those incurred in growing, transporting, marketing, and distributing food—already have been cited. Developed countries must not only end such patterns and habits at home in the name of their own self-interest, but must cease advocating and exporting wasteful practices abroad under the guise of "development, modernization and mechanization."

These benign forms of consumption and waste by developed nations and affluent peoples constitute, however, only a part of the picture. There are also more malevolent forms of consumption and consumerism, whether intentional or not, which must cease as a prerequisite to a just and humane solution to problems of famine and poverty. These include the net, *de facto* export of scarce investment capital—obtained initially from host governments and local private investors—from developing to affluent nations in the form of excessive, non-invested profits for western-based multinational corporations. These also include control by such corporations, by western governments, and by private investors of valuable lands and production facilities in developing countries, lands which are utilized in the production of goods and services for western consumers rather than for the indigenous host population. Such over-consumption of capital, natural resources, labor, and industry in developing countries by western interests constitutes a more sinister and troubling form of waste and profligacy which must be understood, exposed, and terminated.

III. PERSUASION VERSUS COERCION: THE MORAL DILEMMA OF SELECTIVE ALLOCATION

But can these critical objectives—a rationally-reduced demand for an adequate, attainable supply of precious commodities and resources—be achieved through the methods outlined in the preceding two sections? "No chance," says ecologist Garrett Hardin. Persuasive measures must give way to a system of "mutual coercion, mutually agreed upon." Human beings are indolent, complacent and selfish, and will react too late to crises and shortages unless forced by some means to do otherwise.[31]

Is the Good then Good?

Both donative and development strategies, say proponents of selective allocation, represent the best possible intentions producing the worst possible results. All donative schemes, as well as development strategies which focus on supply and ignore the problem of excessive demand, artifically interfere with the natural life cycle, permitting populations in afflicted countries to exceed the "carrying capacity" of their environments. Thus, instead of the natural equilibrium normally established between population growth and the limits of a given environment, donative and development assistance create a "ratchet effect"; temporarily postponing disaster for the present—but at the expense of permanent and irreparable damage to the environment, causing the inevitable human disaster to be all the more tragic and massive in the end. Thus, such forms of assistance are not only ill-advised from a practical standpoint, they are ultimately immoral as well.[32] This is the delicate point and disturbing claim which Mssrs. Fletcher, Englehardt, and Hardin articulate in the present volume.

Dale Runge, doctoral student of M.I.T. Professor Jay Forrester ("Limits to Growth" project) apparently concurs. In an unpublished paper entitled, "The Ethics of Humanitarian Food Relief," Runge argues with the aid of computer simulations that donative and development relief are "not ethical" because by themselves they create more misery over the long run than they alleviate—leading Wade Green of the *New York Times* to wonder, "Is the good then good?"[33]

Philip Handler, president of the National Academy of Sciences, while declaring himself a non-believer in the concept of "triage," does share some of the pessimism of selective allocation advocates. "Cruel as it may sound," he concludes, "if the developed and affluent nations do not intend the colossal, all-out effort commensurate with this task, then it may be wiser to 'let nature take its course'."[34]

Michael Malloy of the *National Observer* speculates that, in part, the current preoccupation with selective allocation proposals may be a reaction in developed countries to both the World Population Conference (Bucharest, Rumania; August 1974) and the World Food Conference in Rome (November 1974). On both occasions developing countries (for reasons cited earlier) refused even to address the population question, and instead passed resolutions condemning developed nations, who "consume too much and give away too little."[35]

Be that as it may, it is important also to recognize that, far from being mere proposals, selective allocation procedures are frequently *practiced* in dealing with many present programs. Title I of the U. S. "Food for Peace" program, as I mentioned earlier, is a case in point. The allocation and distribution of excess food supplies according to a formula based solely on American foreign policy objectives is, quite clearly, a form of selective allocation. While Joseph Fletcher's point may be true, that "it is unrealistic to suppose that allocative reasoning will take place without some thought by those in charge as to the political benefits to be gained," it is also fair to point out that the U. S. has *decried* such activity by *other* nations (such as the OPEC countries) as "political blackmail."[37]

Choices and Policies

The debate raging over triage and lifeboat ethics proposals is clearly much more than a mere disagreement over the most appropriate "metaphor" to describe the current global situation. Rather the importance of this debate is its potential to influence political choice and the formulation of guidelines for future public and foreign policy. Such choices and policies depend upon a fundamental resolution of some of the basic questions raised in the preceding discussion.

Is the "demographic transition theory," for example, an adequate explanation of the complex relationships between population growth and average socio-economic status, or do the "success stories" of low-income nations such as Hong Kong, Singapore, Taiwan, and South Korea argue for a different theory—and for a sterner response? Are idealistic humanitarianism and a kind of selfless altruism (as implied in the Christian concept of *agape*) the only appropriate bases for famine assistance? Or does enlightened self-interest—an exalted form of "moral egoism"—ultimately provide (as the British philosopher Henry Sidgwick argued years ago[38]) a more universally acceptable and practical foundation for moral behavior and political choice? And if so, would the latter conclusion sanction the brand of hard-nosed, *quid pro quo* policies for which Fletcher, Englehardt, and Hardin argue in these pages? Are the profligate habits and the affluency of western nations irrelevant to the issues under discussion as Fletcher and Hardin will argue? Or is western affluence in large part the result of the unjust "consumption" and appropriation of capital and other resources from impoverished countries—a process of economic imperialism which, like uncontrolled population growth, is also a causative factor in the permanent state of economic dependency which characterizes many third-world nations? The resolution of such questions profoundly affects the appropriate choices from among the strategies I have outlined in this essay—and indeed, is likewise significant for a choice among the alternatives which Professor Sellers details, concerning the present moral quality and future moral perceptions of the American people and their nation.

Irrespective of individual positions, I am confident that most persons can be won to the thrust of implications in the present essay; that in the future a carefully managed improvement in the quality and distribution (*rather* than the quantity) of food supplies must be accompanied by an overall reduction of world food demand, accomplished through a cessation both of population growth in *all* nations and of excessive consumption in affluent countries. The disturbing question we now face is whether these goals can be accomplished through the hodgepodge of donative and development strategies I have outlined here, or whether the time indeed has come for a humanitarianly-motivated, coercive policy of selective allocation, as advocated by Garrett Hardin and others. The substantial debate on that critical question occupies the pages which follow.

NOTES

1. Jagdish N. Bhagwati, "Economics and World Order from the 1970's to the 1990's: The Key Issues," in J. N. Bhagwati (editor), *Economics and World Order* (New York: Free Press, 1972) pp. 5, 17.
2. Cf. Paul Ehrlich's comment early in 1971 that "millions of people are going to starve to death before this decade is out." Preface to the revised edition of *The Population Bomb* (New York: Ballantine Books, 1971). See also the somewhat apolitical, "conflict-free" model of global finitude presented in D. H. Meadows, D. L. Meadows, J. Randers and W. Behrens, *The Limits to Growth: A Report for the Club of Rome's Project on the Predicament of Mankind* (New York: Universe Books, 1972).

3. See, for example, Garrett Hardin, "Lifeboat Ethics: The Case Against Helping the Poor," *Psychology Today* (September, 1974); "Living on a Lifeboat," *Bioscience* (October, 1974); "Another Face of Bioethics: The Case for Massive 'Diebacks' of Population," *Modern Medicine 65* (March 1, 1975). See also Johnson C. Montgomery, "The Island of Plenty," *Newsweek* (December 13, 1974), 13. Cf. the proposals for food triage offered in the mid-1960's by Paul and William Paddock: *Famine—1975!* (Boston: Little, Brown and Co., 1967). Cf. also Garrett Hardin's highly anthologized article written at this time: "The Tragedy of the Commons," *Science 162* (December 13, 1968) 1243-48, as well as his later controversial book, *Exploring New Ethics for Survival: The Voyage of the Spaceship Beagle* (New York: Viking Press, 1972).
4. Garrett Hardin, "Living on a Lifeboat," 561, 562, 564. Cf. also "Another Face of Bioethics," and an earlier editorial, "Ecological Conservatism," *Chemical and Engineering News 49*, 28 (July 12, 1971).
5. Cf. Lester Brown and Erik Eckholm, *By Bread Alone* (New York: Praeger Publishers, 1974) pp. 65-67. For a brief but excellent discussion of the origins and "faulty economics" of the "Food for Peace" program, see Laurence J. Hewes, Jr., "U. S. Short Term Food Policy Alternatives," *Center Report* (April, 1975) 7-9.
6. Lester R. Brown, *World without Borders* (New York: Vintage Books, 1973), pp. 314-16. Brown and Eckholm, pp. 227-28. See also Brown and Eckholm, "Next Steps Toward Global Food Security," in J. W. Howe, *et al.*, *The U. S. and World Development: Agenda for Action, 1975* (New York: Praeger Publishers and the Overseas Development Council, 1975) p. 81.
7. The more recent "fourth world" designation has evolved in response to the growing discrepancy between some "third world" countries (such as Brazil, South Korea, Taiwan and the OPEC countries) which have exhibited marked improvements in their national economies and basic standard of living, and others (such as India and several of the African nations) which remain largely entrenched in poverty. CF. Helen C. Low and James W. Howe, "Focus on the Fourth World," *The U. S. and World Development*, pp. 35-54.
8. Lester R. Brown, *World without Borders*, p. 96; Brown and Eckholm, *By Bread Alone*, p. 7; L. Brown, *In the Human Interest* (New York: W. W. Norton, 1974) pp. 47–49. Clearly Brown and Eckholm are speaking here of *gross agricultural potential*. Actual increases in the year-to-year net harvest also depend upon a variety of other factors in addition to the four basic resources they list, factors such as climate, pest control, efficiency of harvesting, transportation and marketing methods, and so forth—all of which they discuss at length elsewhere.
9. Brown and Eckholm, *By Bread Alone*, p. 78.
10. Ibid., p. 86. Cf. also Lester Brown, *In the Human Interest*, p. 48.
11. *By Bread Alone*, pp. 8, 92–104.
12. Source: calculations by Prof. Charles C. Bradley, as quoted in *By Bread Alone*, p. 104.
13. Ibid., pp. 104–05; cf. also pp. 9, 107, 108, 110.
14. See Brown and Eckholm, "Next Steps Toward Global Food Security," and *By Bread Alone*, pp. 209–25.
15. Alan Berg, "The Trouble with Triage," *New York Times Magazine*, (June 15, 1975) 28.
16. Source: U. S. Department of Agriculture data (1964); quoted in *By Bread Alone*, p. 118.
17. Brown and Eckholm, *By Bread Alone*, p. 137.

18. *By Bread Alone*, p. 7.
19. Alan Berg, "Industry's Struggle with World Malnutrition," *Harvard Business Review* (January-February, 1972) 130–42.
20. Elizabeth Mann Borgese, "The Blue Revolution: Harvesting the Fruits of the Sea," *Center Report* (April, 1975) 18–19. Cf. also an earlier article, "The Drama of Oceans," *Center Report* (October, 1973) 21–23.
21. Brown and Eckholm, "Next Steps Toward Global Food Security," p. 78.
22. Paul Ehrlich, op. cit. See Also Paul and Anne Ehrlich, *Population, Resources, Environment: Issues in Human Ecology,* rev. ed. (San Francisco: W. H. Freeman & Co., 1972). A partial list of Prof. Hardin's most recent publications devoted specifically to population includes: "Ten Charming Delusions About Population," *American Biology Teacher* (February, 1975) 102–03; "Nobody Ever Dies of Overpopulation," *Science 171*, 3971 (February 12, 1971), 527; "Preserving Quality on Spaceship Earth," (speech before the Mexico City Conference on North American Wildlife and National Resources, March 12–15, 1972), published by the Wildlife Management Institute (Washington, D.C.); "Another Face of Bioethics: The Case for Massive 'Diebacks' of Population," loc. cit.; "Rights, Human and Nonhuman: The Rational Basis of Conservation," *North American Review* (Winter, 1974) 14–17.
23. See the comments by Dr. Stuart Hinds of the World Health Organization in G. R. Lucas, Jr. (ed.), *Triage in Medicine and Society* (Houston: Institute of Religion, 1975) pp. 52–53. This is not true, however, of *all* regions within India. Cf. Alan Berg, "The Trouble with Triage," loc. cit., p. 31.
24. Lester Brown, *In the Human Interest*, p. 119 (emphases added). Cf. "The Socioeconomic Threshold," pp. 140–41 in *World without Borders*.
25. See Prof. Hardin's recent editorial, "Gregg's Law," in *Bioscience 25*, 7 (July, 1975), 415. Cf. Dr. Fletcher's remarks in my *Triage in Medicine and Society*, pp. 28–29. See also Dr. Hardin's testimony before H. R. Subcommittee on Fisheries and Wildlife Conservation and the Environment: *Growth and its Implications* (Washington, D.C.: U. S. Government Printing Office, 1975) #93–95, p. 450. Cf. Brown, *In the Human Interest*, p. 154; and *World without Borders*, p. 152.
26. *By Bread Alone*, p. 180.
27. Alan Berg, "The Trouble with Triage," loc. cit., p. 30.
28. Source: FAO Food Balance Sheets (1964–66), and USDA figures in *By Bread Alone*, p. 40. Cf. also the comments on Norway's progress in this regard in Brown and Eckholm, "Next Steps Toward Global Food Security," loc. cit., pp. 79–80. Cf. these in turn with the more recent figures, together with an analysis of their impact in *New York Times*, "Week in Review," Sec. 4, p. 3 (September 28, 1975).
29. For an excellent discussion of these points, see the article by James E. Will: "Understanding the Impact of Worldwide Inequities," *Christian Century* (May 7, 1975) 471–73.
30. Paul Lewis, "The World Economy: Searching for Strength," *New York Times*, Sec. 3, p. 1, (September 14, 1975).
31. It is interesting to note that David Hume, commenting on land reform and the enactment of increasingly severe land conservation policies in Great Britain during his own time, lent substance to Hardin's current argument. Hume argued that it is only *after* commodities become scarce or in short supply—only, in a sense, after it is too late—that we begin to develop a sense of the "ethics" regarding their use. Cf. *An Enquiry Concerning the Principles of Morals* (1751), in C. W. Hendel (ed.), *Hume: Selections* (New York: Charles

Scribners' Sons, 1927) p. 184. Cf. Garrett Hardin, "The Tragedy of the Commons," loc. cit.

32. Garrett Hardin, "Living on a Lifeboat," 563–65. Cf. also Prof. Hardin's testimony before the House Subcommittee on conservation concerns, loc. cit.

33. Wade Green, "Triage: Who Shall be Fed? Who Shall Starve?" *New York Times Magazine* (January 5, 1975), 10.

34. Quoted in Michael T. Malloy, " 'Let 'Em Starve!' A New Approach to World Hunger," lead article in *The National Observer* (March 29, 1975) 1, 17. See also Wade Green, "Triage," loc. cit., 44.

35. M. T. Malloy, " 'Let 'Em Starve!'," 27.

36. Cf. also my remarks in conclusion in *Triage in Medicine and Society*, pp. 53–56.

37. G. R. Lucas, Jr., "Famine and Global Policy: An Interview with Joseph Fletcher," *Christian Century* (September 3–10, 1975) 755. Review also the comments in this regard in *Triage in Medicine and Society*: e.g., pp. 31, 34, and 36–56. Also cf. the telling comments by James E. Will, "Understanding the Impact of Worldwide Inequities," and Brown and Eckholm, *By Bread Alone*, pp. 69–72.

38. Henry Sidgwick, *Methods of Ethics*, 7th edition (Cambridge: Cambridge University Press, 1906). [Reissued *inter alia* by the University of Chicago Press, 1962.] Esp. Book I, Ch. VII; Book II; and the "Concluding Chapter."

ON THE RELATIONS OF MEDICAL TRIAGE TO WORLD FAMINE:
An Historical Survey

STUART W. HINDS

N EARLY TWO HUNDRED YEARS AGO Thomas R. Malthus (1766–1834)—a cleric, author, professor of history and political economy, co-founder of the Statistical Society of London, and Fellow of the Royal Society—startled and shocked contemporary society with the views and theories he published anonymously in a pamphlet entitled, "An Essay on the Principles of Population, as it affects the Future Improvement of Society, with remarks on the speculations of Mr. Godwin, M. Condorcet and Others."[1] In subsequent editions of "The Essay" (now swollen to a full size book bearing his name) he developed his theory further, arguing that infinite human hopes for social happiness must be vain, for population would always tend to outstrip the growth of production, and while population growth, if unchecked, would grow geometrically, the means of subsistence would only advance by arithmetical progression.

Though Malthus' views had an immediate effect on the thinkers of his day (Charles Darwin [1809–1882], for instance, referred to the work as "perhaps the most important book I read"[2]), few people really believed the position presently facing

Dr. Hinds, a former Royal Air Force medical officer, is a pediatrician, medical historian, and a Member of the Royal College of Physicians. He has taught over the years on the medical and public health faculties of the Universities of London, Bristol, Michigan, and Texas, and at universities in Turkey, Poland, Sweden, Yugoslovia, and Greece. He has been a consultant and advisor for the World Health Organization since 1955.

the world would ever become a reality. A few years after the appearance of the sixth and last edition in 1826, the work was all but forgotten.

Alarmed by the growing numbers facing malnutrition, hunger, and starvation, the present century has witnessed an awakening interest in the Malthusian theory. Since the mid-thirties, growing numbers of scientists, humanists, scientific bodies, government agencies, and governments themselves have met repeatedly to examine the problem of widespread hunger and to find a solution to the worsening situation. In spite of a mounting volume of articles, books, and official reports, both scientific[3] and governmental,[4] comparatively little impact has been made on the ever-mounting crisis.

In 1946 the Nobel-laureate Boyd-Orr (1880–1971), an accepted world authority on nutrition and food supply problems and a founder and first director of the United Nations Food and Agriculture Organization, called an emergency conference in Washington, D. C. to examine the advancing threat of post war famine. A special council was established to distribute food to each nation according to its needs and not its purchasing power, a move which averted the immediate threat of world-wide famine at that time. Boyd-Orr's proposal to establish a permanent World Food Board, however, was defeated by American and British opposition. Resigning from the F. A. O. in 1948, he worked relentlessly in organizations seeking to establish a world government. During his lifetime he published *Food and the People* (1936), *Food—The Foundation of World Unity* (1943), *The White Man's Dilemma* (1948), and *Food and Famine* (1960) with a great many papers on the subject besides—most of them now already forgotten.

At the present time it is not possible to count the cost in human suffering and degradation wrought by famine which has occurred already, is taking place at this very moment, and will go on taking place minute by minute, hour by hour, day by day, and year by year, until very probably the turn of the next century. There are now those, however, who advocate turning a blind eye to the plight of the multitudes of starving and famine-ridden peoples by applying the principles referred to as "triage." (The phrase "social triage" is employed frequently in this regard.) The term "triage" has until recently been used to refer to a strictly medical procedure. It has now come dramatically to the forefront in contemporary discussions of famine and over-population.

I

ORIGINS AND HISTORY OF MEDICAL TRIAGE

The *Oxford English Dictionary*[5] shows the word to have originated in the fourteenth century from the French "triere" meaning "to pick, select, choose or cull." It defined triage as "picking or sorting according to quality" (my emphases). Examples of its use included:

1. the selection of pelts according to quality:
    Each fleece consists of wool of diverse qualities and degrees of fineness which the dealers therein take to separate. If the triage or separation be well made, in 15 bales there will be . . . (*Chambers Cycl. S.V. Wool.* 1727–1741);

2. separation of broken beans from whole beans:
    These (pickers) sort the (coffee) berries into three classes; best quality, middling and the third of all, the bad broken berries is called "triage coffee" (*The Gentleman's Magazine*, 1825. XCV. 216);

3. An advertisement in the *London Daily News* in 1880 ran:
    "Coffee—Costa Rica—Triage 59s.6d."

Thus a prominent use of the word in the eighteenth and nineteenth centuries was to denote the sorting or sifting of coffee beans into three grades, the lowest of which, containing the broken beans gathered up off the warehouse floor and packaged, was sold as "triage." *Webster's Dictionary*[6] likewise cites references to "sorting, sifting and selecting," "the grading of marketable produce," and "the lowest grade of coffee berries consisting of broken material"—and then, almost as an afterthought: "The sorting of battle casualties for first aid at collecting stations at the front, before their evacuation to hospitals in the rear."

Three standard medical dictionaries,[7] all published in the United States of America, contain the term, while *The British Medical Dictionary*,[8] having more than 100 specialist contributors, does not list "triage." An acceptable definition follows:

"*French: sorting.* The medical screening of patients to determine their priority for treatment. The sorting of casualties in military and civil disasters into three groups: those who will be expected to survive regardless of treatment, those who will be expected to die regardless of what is done for them, and those who will die *unless* given immediate aid."[9]

The system of sorting casualties and assigning priorities according to their medical and surgical needs was first devised and perfected on the battlefield by Baron Domineque Jean Larrey (1766–1842), Surgeon-in-Chief of the Imperial Armies of the Emperor Napoleon and Inspector General of the Medical Staff of the French Armies. He was an outstanding surgeon and a reformer of medical services for armies in peacetime and in war, as well as an inventor, teacher, historian, ornithologist, and philanthropist. He served the Emperor unswervingly throughout his life, and the French Armies for over half a century. Present at some sixty battles and four hundred lesser engagements, he always showed marked fortitude and great bravery under fire, giving of his best skill to friend and foe alike without thought of his own safety.

Horrified by the suffering and the great loss of life for the want of medical care on the battlefield, Larrey, early in his military career designed and introduced the "ambulance volante." this was a two and four wheeled horse-drawn vehicle, well sprung and easily maneuverable, used to collect the wounded even at the height of battle after emergency medical and surgical care had been given on the field of battle. His plan was to provide full surgical care where the wounded lay, even at this preanesthetic time, and to remove all casualties rapidly to a place of safety after treatment had been undertaken.

To appreciate the novelty of his innovation, one has only to realize that traditionally the wounded were left to lie on the field until the battle was over, at which time the local inhabitants would be expected to tend the dead and the dying as best they could. One need only review accounts of the major battles of the American Civil War, long after Larrey's time, to realize how many men died as the result of a lack of adequate and timely medical care at the front lines.

Larrey proposed that medical services must be provided during and not after a battle.

"... those who are dangerously wounded must be tended first, entirely without regard to rank or distinction. Those less severely injured must wait until the gravely wounded have been operated upon and dressed. The slightly wounded may go to the hospital in the first or second line; especially the officers, since they have horses and therefore have transport—and regardless, most of these have but trivial wounds.[10]

This would seem to be the first reference to the system now routine in modern military and civilian medical "sorting." The word "triage" is not employed by Larrey, nor is there any indication that he used precisely this term in establishing the principles of modern military casualty medicine. It is important to recognize, however, that Larrey rejected out of hand any idea of treating persons by priorities other than medical need.

The word "triage" does not feature in the indexes of either *Military Surgeon* (93 volumes),[11] or *Military Medicine* (25 volumes),[12] the two journals devoted exclusively to military medicine. Nor does the word "triage" appear in any articles dealing with war casualties, the evacuation of casualties, first aid, treatment of battle casualties, or casualty treatment in either publication. Instead, the words "sorting," "selection," "selective tagging," and so forth are used throughout.

Nor is the word found in the index of any of the fourteen volumes of *The History of the Second World War* (British),[13] but it does appear some twenty times in the index of the equivalent *American History*. In volume II, *Surgery in World War II* (in a chapter entitled, "Activities of Surgical Consultants"), the word is used in the text as a noun, a verb, and as an adjective. Brigadier Porritt, Consulting Surgeon to the British 21st Army Group, having been asked to open a discussion on "sorting," observed: "Sorting I must prefer to triage."[14]

Later at the first Interallied Consultants Conference, held on the 15th of October, 1944, General Mouro, Consulting Surgeon to the British Army on the subject of sorting remarked:

> "The word 'triage' has been quite rightfully condemned. I think it is outlived, and some more sensible word such as grouping, or selection is the word of choice. I don't think it matters very much that we have three groups a, b and c or one, two and three. That after all, is intended only as a guide for one who hasn't faced it before. It is as Brigadier Porritt said, common sense that matters."[15]

Sorting or "medical triage" thus historically has meant the classification and sorting of casualties (both those physically injured or wounded) and the sick (from whatever cause) into priority groups according to their individual needs, without reference to rank, birth, or favor. When for any reason shortages of essential facilities complicate the picture, the sorting will be influenced further by the prognosis rating of each casualty.

This is precisely what Baron Larrey said two hundred years ago.

Accurate assessment of need, allocation of priorities, and a considered prognosis—combined with speed, lucid thinking, and firm decisions—are the hallmarks of good sorting. In every such situation one presupposes that medical knowledge is adequate to gauge the effects and the consequences of each and every "triage" decision.

Situations calling for this type of medical action are commonly of short duration, what one would call disasters: road, train, aircraft and industrial accidents, explosions, fires, and sudden acute illnesses or epidemics. These end with the disposal of the casualties according to the decisions made for their care. Seldom does a situation of this type last longer than a few hours, or perhaps days. The aim of the entire operation is to save life and limb, to reduce suffering, and to provide appropriate treatment to aid recovery in as short a time as possible. This routine sorting of casualties into priority groups according to their needs is in some quarters referred to as "medical triage" or the "triage process." The person making the selection is then referred to as the "triage officer," and if this be a nurse, the "triage nurse." Casualties who have been processed or sorted by this system may be described as having been "triaged," and the place where a sorting was carried out, as a "triage site."

WARTIME ENCOUNTERS WITH MEDICAL TRIAGE

A crisis situation needing sensitive decisions and showing the difficulties which frequently were encountered (one of many such incidents occurring in the North African campaign during World War II) involved a British plane which crashed in the western desert some hundred miles from the only road which hugged the coast line all the way to Alexandria, several hundred miles to the east. The crew were badly injured and some severely burned. Only four doses of morphia were available, inadequate to meet the needs of the occasion, since a similar crash of an enemy plane the previous day had depleted the meager stock. To which of the casualties should the available morphine be given?

Men as severely injured as these needed urgent treatment which could only be obtained at the base hospital several hundred miles away. Transport was therefore crucial; but with shortages of the kinds common at this time, the one ambulance available had no engine under the hood and needed to be towed by another vehicle. The only plane that could be used was too small to fly out more than half of the number of casualties—and then only when the injured had been moved to a local landing ground. The decisions faced by the medical officer on this occasion (myself) included: to which of the injured should the available morphine be given, to which the space on the plane, and to which should either or both be denied? No other decisions or alternatives were possible.

A totally different situation involving a "triage"-type decision arose when a night fighter squadron took over a lately-abandoned enemy landing strip near Tobruk. The strip was virtually a tiny oasis in a large enemy mine field with limited areas of access. Night fighter pilots took off and landed with only a minimum of light—a necessity in "night fighting." It seemed entirely possible that an occasion might arise when a damaged plane, unable to land in the limited space, would crash in the surrounding mine field. The question arose as to what the rescue procedure should be if such an eventuality occurred, especially since the ambulance driver, the squadron medical officer, and the nursing orderlies were the only medical personnel in the area, and since the medical care of the entire unit rested in their hands. Should the team "go in" and risk itself in order to attempt a rescue, or should we await the arrival of a team of "sappers" to clear the way to the downed plane? The commanding officer, when approached for his view, could only respond: "Doc, I haven't any idea at all. Do what you think is right."

It might be questioned whether this was a canonical case of "medical triage"—but in a sense it clearly was. A decision had to be made between risking the lives of the only available team and the lives of a two-man crew somewhere in a mine field in the darkness.

Henry Beecher, a distinguished physician and medical scholar at Harvard University, has discussed the use of penicillin in those early days following its availability during World War II. He described one controversial situation as follows:

> When the wonders of penicillin were new, but recognized, and the supply heartbreakingly meager, a small shipment finally arrived in North Africa during World War II. The hospital beds were overflowing with wounded men. Many had been wounded in battles; many had also been wounded in brothels. Which group would get

the penicillin? By all that is just, it would go to the heroes who had risked their lives, who were still in jeopardy, and some of whom were dying. They did not receive it, nor should they have; it was given to those infected in brothels. Before indignation takes over, let us examine the situation. First, there were desperate shortages of manpower at the front. Second, those with broken bodies and broken bones would not be swiftly restored to the battle line even with penicillin, whereas those with venereal disease, on being treated with penicillin, would in a matter of days free the beds they were occupying and return to the front.[16]

Clearly this was the correct decision to make. At this time the possibility of contracting venereal disease at the front, deep in the western desert, did not exist. As the army grew in manpower, however, as many men as could be spared during the long lulls in the fighting were granted leave. These returned to the Allied base in the delta for much needed rest and refreshment. Some of these men contracted infections—as did some of the new replacements from Britain and elsewhere who were awaiting posting to combatant units. The selective use of small supplies of penicillin available to fit these men for duty was completely justifiable on a number of grounds. For instance, adequate re-serves of fresh personnel for replacement gave war weary and wounded men the opportunity of much needed rest. In addition units could be maintained at full strength by a quick return to duty of men who were fit in every other way but for a venereal infection, which would respond quickly to penicillin.

An unusual incident, directly involved with the "penicillin triage" policy, may be of interest. In England in 1944 (at the time of the opening of the "second front") the same directive concern-ing the use of penicillin was in effect for those charged with the care of men involved in that crucial invasion of Europe. Pilots and other air crew who previously had flown in other kinds of aircraft were during this period selected and posted to "heavy bomber conversion units" in England for some weeks. Here they were "crewed up" and trained to man the large bombers used to carry the offensive deep into Europe.

It took several weeks to train a crew to operate these large aircraft. If one member of a crew dropped out or fell ill during the training, the entire crew would be disabled until the sick man was fit to resume training. If a man was likely to be absent for any length of time, a replacement was found—but it meant that the entire crew would have to start the course over again. The rationale of "penicillin triage" described by Beecher was, therefore, obvious: the sick crew member could be returned to training after treatment lasting only two days. Physicians treating aircrew suffering from gonorrhea in the station sick quarters believed it was justifiable to regard these men as having priority use of the limited supply of penicillin in order that the reserve of essential replacement bomber crews be maintained—particularly when adequate supplies of sulphonamides and other drugs were available and were often as effective (and in many cases the treatment of choice) for other conditions.

Yet even this clearly acceptable policy was not without its moments of conflict. In the midst of this penicillin program one of the enlisted personnel (not a crew member) developed an enormous carbuncle, involving the entire left side of his neck and spreading over his shoulder and partway down his arm. Every treatment (save penicillin) was tried in order to arrest the spread of this deadly infection, but to no avail.

When it became obvious that this man's condition was worsening, it was thought that penicillin might offer a last resort. We therefore decided to list this patient in the medical files as having contracted venereal disease, so that treatment with penicillin could be attempted. Having obtained his consent to mark his medical service record in this manner, he was given one of the precious vials of penicillin. He began to improve, and ultimately made a complete recovery. In my experience, somewhat in contrast to the statement of the problem by Beecher, this was the only instance where a man's life and well-being actually were threatened by the penicillin triage policy. And it was a situation, as well as a conflict, which we were able to resolve successfully.

In the events described, shortages of one type or another existed: drugs, medical supplies, surgical equipment, blood for transfusion, transportation, as well as many other items. By careful management the effect of shortages could often be minimized and the quandary of "selective allocation" to some extent reduced. Unforeseen emergencies and sudden, unexpected catastrophes—indeed any event giving rise to many casualties—would exacerbate the problem. These emergencies were usually of short duration, however, commonly lasting minutes to a few hours; but occasionally it was a day or so before the wounded could be evacuated safely to places for adequate medical treatment.

TRIAGE IN CONTEMPORARY MEDICINE

In any disaster some kind of initial sorting must be attempted.
Sorting of this nature is practiced routinely in civil life. For
example, the injured, having been sorted into priorities at the
site of the disaster, may be sent to hospitals where the equipment, supplies, and personnel may be insufficient to meet the
needs. Some kind of selection or division to establish priority for
treatment must therefore be made there as well. Treatment is
given first to those who are judged to be in danger of their lives,
but who also have a reasonable chance of recovery. The less
severely injured must wait, and the clearly hopeless cases (difficult as it always is to accept) must be left to die quietly.

During an epidemic, what may be referred to as a "three color
warning system" is put into practice by hospitals in many countries. It is a system of sorting patients for priority admission to
those hospitals. A "red alert" means that all hospitals are alerted
to reserve as many beds as possible for the special cases. Thus
"triage" decisions are made at a national or city level in times of
emergency. In this fashion persons of greatest risk and need can
be ensured admission and given priority treatment. Meanwhile,
an attempt is made to reduce the number at risk by immunizing
the fit priority groups, and by giving these groups first access to
vaccines and any other measures which may be available.

A system of selective hospital admissions, based solely on the
urgency of individual medical needs, has been normal practice
for a very long time in Britain and in other countries. People
with potentially serious conditions, even on suspicion only, are
admitted at once, while all others may be placed on a waiting
list—the length of wait before admission depending largely on
the availability of hospital beds and the nature of the individual
condition. Any unanticipated worsening of a person's condition
while awaiting admission brings an earlier or even immediate
admission. Such a system is no more or no less than a rational
application of an acceptable and accepted selection or "triage"
process, which must always be used when scarcities exist.

The same selective process is used to distribute other essentials
temporarily in short supply. In 1952, for example, when Salk
polio vaccine was in short supply, the British government was
persuaded to purchase a consignment of the new vaccine. The
allotment fell far short of the amount required to vaccinate every

child in Great Britain. Only the year before Denmark had had an outbreak of one of the most severe types of poliomyelitis with a high incidence of serious complications. Parents with young children were dreading the coming of the Autumn of 1953 and the possibility of the spread of the severe disease to Britain. The Ministry of Health decided, therefore, that to make this consignment of polio vaccine go around most equitably, all eligible children would have their names listed for a lottery-type selection. Children of a certain age, born in a certain month (much like the former draft lottery in America) were chosen at random to receive the vaccine. Almost every family had eligible children who were not selected for vaccination.

This is "triage." It is accepted in such medical contexts —indeed, would any reasonably-minded person have it otherwise?

II

FAMINE AND POPULATION

The tempo of the world's population growth began to increase dramatically after 1650 A.D. Since that date it has been accelerating relentlessly decade after decade, until in 1970 it has reached the stupendous rate of seventy to seventy-five million persons a year—and the rate continues to grow. In the past fifty years, most of the growth has taken place in the nations of the "third world." Why?

It is not possible to provide a full and adequate treatment of this problem in this brief essay—nor should it be necessary, since responsible demographers and sociologists have devoted a great deal of attention to this question in recent years.[17] Yet for all this discussion it is ironic to note that the tacit and implicit premise in all current discussions of triage and lifeboat ethics procedures is that the present population explosion is due simply and solely to the irresponsible fecundity of the poor!

Let us for the moment be willing hypothetically to accept all the pejorative judgments in this regard which have been leveled at the underprivileged populations, in western countries as well as in the third world—that they are habitually lazy, selfish, irresponsibly fecund, and so forth. One would have to proceed from these judgments, however, to the logical observation that these conditions must have existed from time immemorial, whereas the population explosion is, in the third world at least, a comparatively recent phenomenon. That is to say, poor people have not suddenly and inexplicably learned how to reproduce! Thus these pejorative and frequently uninformed judgments about improverished persons, even if accepted, do not themselves offer an adequate explanation of the population crisis.

The present population problem clearly is not due solely to excessive fecundity, but is rather attributable to a number of complex and highly significant events in history. For this reason it is necessary to preface any further discussion of triage and lifeboat ethics with a very brief review of certain events during the last three and one-half centuries, with an especially close scrutiny of the past fifty years. To my mind the findings seem to suggest that the very nations which are currently entertaining the possibility of withholding food from the starving have themselves played a large and frequently a crucial part, not only in bringing the population explosion about, but indeed in ensuring that it would occur.

In nature all living things co-exist in an exquisitely balanced ecological state. The balance, though sensitive and easily upset by an almost limitless number of differing events, is inherently self-stabilizing (though the new balance well may be quite a different situation from whatever had existed previous to such an upset).

The human population as part of the global ecological system, has always been culled by natural events and disasters —droughts, floods, typhoons, tidal waves, and all manner of pestilences (including that disease generic to humanity alone; namely, war). In particular there have always been periods of famine as far back as one might care to go in recorded history, and even before (as the evidence turned up by the archeologists' spades and brushes frequently suggests).

In the eighteenth and nineteenth centuries, however, the traditional agrarian communities of the western world for the first time gave way extensively to urban and industrial societies. This in turn brought immense changes to social and economic patterns of life; on one hand, increased hazards from urban overcrowding and industrial pollution; on the other hand, increased income, stability, and job security for laborers, including children, to man the factories. The concomitant industrial and technological revolution stimulated a rapid increase in the demand for and consumption of all types of manufactured goods. Against this background the present patterns of western fertility and mortality were formed, and were, as the historical records indicate, accompanied by a population explosion. During this ciritical period, for instance, the population of England rose suddenly from nine to thirty-six million persons, two and one-half of whom emigrated to other nations. If all the peoples of the world in the nineteenth century had multiplied at the same rate as did England and Wales, the world population in 1900 would have been close to four billion; instead, it was only 1.6 billion.[18]

The current population explosion in the rest of the developing world likewise has come from the sudden introduction of certain modern technologies into underdeveloped and frequently unprepared agrarian nations. These changes often have been accomplished without sufficient "lead time" for cultural readjustment, and without the equivalent economic and social changes which had taken place in the west during its industrial revolution.

In a sense then the rest of the world is only now beginning to "catch up" with our population explosion. In the west the changes came about relatively slowly, however (on the order of two hundred years), whereas in the developing nations such changes have been rapid indeed (more on the order of fifty years).

In addition, since the early years of the present century, a new factor has appeared and intervened increasingly to upset the balance of nature and to bring about immense changes in the life of mankind. In this instance the reaction has been catastrophic.

By the end of World War II the more advanced countries had developed and largely perfected (in response to many of the problems met with during the war) a wide variety of highly sophisticated drugs and medical techniques in the areas of both preventive and curative medicine such as had never been possible before. Flushed with the newly acquired power to control scourges which hitherto had killed scores of millions of men, women, and children every year, these new techniques were carried to the peoples of the developing countries under the auspices of national and international organizations. Teams of experts descended upon these new countries, offering them "the wonders of western medicine": pesticides, drugs, hospital equipment and hospitals—but above all the means whereby infections, both of the tropics and of the temperate zones, could be controlled and cured as never before.

But the lessons of history and the warnings of Malthus, Boyd-Orr, General Smuts, Toynbee, Stringfellow Barr, Roosevelt, and Labin (to mention a few) were ignored. For whereas disease can be brought under control with potent drugs, pesticides, and the other new techniques, often within a matter of years, traditions and cultural patterns do not change with the same ease or at the same pace, nor do they respond immediately to science.

Immense loss of infant life, for example, was accepted as a way of life in many nations. With higher than average death rates for all other age groups, combined with a low life expectancy, it had become traditional and customary— indeed essential to survival—for these people to have very large families. In due historical course this reproductive pattern had become part of their culture. It was accepted as a good and necessary thing to have a large number of children both to help scratch a living from the soil and to act as an insurance against the needs of the later years of life.

This pattern of child bearing differs little from the patterns which existed in western countries during the middle ages, indeed, right up to the early years of the twentieth century. Families of ten to fourteen children were commonplace in Britain even at the turn of the century.

The Primary Education Act of 1870, however, greatly influenced family size in England. Until that date large numbers of children, as I have already indicated, helped to maintain the family economy by being engaged in cottage industries, or else laboring in the fields, factories, or mines. Both Daniel Defoe (1660–1731)[19] and William Cobbett (1763–1835)[20] in their writings mentioned with pride the industrial dexterity shown by the children of their times.

But with compulsory attendance at school and the beginnings of some control on the hours children were allowed to work, the large family became a financial liability rather than an asset, contributing greatly toward the desire for smaller families. Though contraceptive literature and techniques to practice family limitation became available about the same time (1870) in both the United States and Britain—and indeed attracted much interest—many families still tended to be large (six, eight, ten, and even a dozen children not being unusual until the early years of the twentieth century). Infant mortality meanwhile showed little tendency to fall in spite of steadily improving environmental conditions until the dramatic discoveries in the medicine of comparatively recent times—this even though the massive killers of the tropics were wholly absent in the temperate zones.

Thus, only in the last few years can the West be said to have recovered and re-established comparative equilibrium following the industrial revolution, which began some two hundred years ago!

In the developing countries, many of them within the tropical and subtropical zones, an agrarian economy with small farms and family industries still largely exists. Schools and schooling vary from inadequate to nonexistent, illiteracy is almost universal, and housing and sanitary conditions are still primitive. Until the last twenty-five years disease (both exotic tropical conditions and the more mundane conditions found the world over) took a terrible toll of life, most especially of infants and children. The belief still lingers therefore that the wealth of a family can be measured by the number of living children, and in certain countries the importance of male children to perform filial rites at the father's funeral is still of vital concern.

The importance of this reproductive pattern—the result of centuries of struggle against fearful odds and now deeply ingrained in these cultures—was not adequately considered when the remarkable medical advances were taken to underdeveloped societies in the early years immediately after the last war. More important by far would have been a massive plan to share agricultural expertise with these people, together with basic educational programs. From the beginning all aid in the medical field should have given top priority to family limitation to indicate its importance in modern medical thinking. Instead the emphasis has been on control and cure of disease with minimal help in both the educational and agricultural fields. The policy should have been one of progressive aid to help these people to help themselves and to fit themselves into the rapidly-changing world of the twentieth century.[21]

In the early 1960's I had occasion to travel through Turkey on behalf of the World Health Organization in order to aid the establishment of a comprehensive, pre-paid health service for the country. A number of the local women had heard, quite erroneously, that I had come in fact as a bearer of "the pill." Hearing this rumor, they downed their hoes and spades; they ignored the fact that they were Turkish, Kurd, and Armenian women who, under rigid social custom, do not speak with strange men. They ignored every conventional social and cultural taboo in order to ask me, even beg me, to bring oral contraceptives to the women of Eastern Turkey.

When I questioned them about the strength of their desire, they explained that it was tradition for them to have at the end of their child-bearing period from six to eight living children. To achieve this, they were forced to endure an average of between eighteen to twenty-four pregnancies (so high was the infant mortality rate at that time). No longer content to endure this hardship, they had come to ask for contraceptive aid.

Instances such as this finally succeeded in communicating to us the potential danger inherent in the health services which we proposed to provide. We recognized the threat to this nation's fragile economy and survival capacity should those thousands dying in infancy suddenly be protected and saved for adulthood. As a result, we proceeded first with the dissemination of family planning theories and resources to the entire population. This service then was continued as their national health service began to take form.

Reviewing the demographic and medical data of the Turkish nation over the last dozen years reveals two remarkable facts: mortality rates, particularly in infancy, have declined dramatically, while the total population hardly has grown at all. This was accomplished in a nation where previous custom had dictated an enormous number of pregnancies and births.

In marked contrast to this example, however, the peoples of the newly developing countries, relieved of the burden of the very high infant death rate which has plagued their societies throughout history, now have a far greater number of their children survive to adulthood and enter the reproductive period of life. Today forty to forty-five percent of the population of the underdeveloped countries are under fifteen years of age. Meanwhile the western world stands aghast at the population explosion in these countries, amazed that young adults should wish to reproduce and critical of their inability to recognize the immense problems they are creating, not only for themselves, but also for the rest of the world.

In my opinion it is no exaggeration to say that the western world, by making the advanced preventive and curative techniques available to the peoples of the third world without at the same time making the other really vital twentieth century facilities available to them, must accept much of the responsibility for the present situation.

Now as the "final straw" the world shortage of energy and the dramatic rise in the price of oil has done nothing but harm to the poorer countries, bringing their primitive agricultural practices, already severely hit by quite unusual weather conditions, to a precipitate end. Shortages of oil and replacement parts for tractors, which were purchased to replace the beasts which had pulled the ploughs for centuries (and had provided a little manure for fertilizer besides), together with the prohibitive rise in the cost of artificial fertilizer, water shortages, and lack of good seed, all have reduced the ability of the poor nations even to provide the bare necessities for themselves.

Finally, in relating the problems of population to those of famine there exist certain convincing arguments with a ring of the ironic that has become all too familiar.

Everyone knows just how many pounds of grain are needed to produce one pound of beef. Incredibly this grain is actually fed to an animal which is already the most efficient producer of beef through the consumption of foods which are totally inedible to man. Millions of human beings are starving and dying hourly for want of a minimum quantity of the very grain now being fed uselessly to cattle in the United States. While kine chew a grain cud to provide beef for an already overfed people, others starve to death. In other ways, as has been pointed out by Miles:

> One American consumes some 30 times as much oil and scarce minerals as a Pakistani . . . and even a comparatively slow rate of population growth in the United States may have as deleterious a long range effect on man's total environment as 10, 20, or 30 times faster growth of an equivalent population in low consumption agrarian economies.[22]

Surely the western world cannot now stand idly by, withdraw within its boundaries, and from that safe vantage point suggest that the answer to the population explosion lies in the application of "social" or "food triage." We have been warned repeatedly for the past two centuries about famine and population growth, and perhaps no more dramatically than when Lord Boyd-Orr's proposal to establish a World Food Board was passed over by the American and British governments.

MEDICAL AND SOCIAL TRIAGE

To the vast majority of peoples in the world, the word "triage" is unknown and meaningless, while elsewhere it enjoys a very limited use. When it has been used and where it may be used today with a medical connotation, it has meant the allocation of priority according to need, and on no other grounds, for goods and services in short supply. The word thus conjures up a vision of selflessness, aid, and life saving services in the best tradition of medicine, bringing limited medical and social resources to those needing it most. When "triage" is qualified by the word "social," an even more benevolent, kindly, and helpful sense may come to mind: the kind of understanding and help given in times of stress, illness, or misfortune. The image no doubt comes from years of use of such phrases as "social services," "social security," and "social conscience."

What "triage" means today is quite the reverse. In the "lifeboat ethics" context "social triage" means sorting on social grounds—not to benefit or give of goods in short supply to the most needy, but the very opposite: to divert goods and food from those who have been sorted on social grounds and found wanting for whatever reason. As has been indicated, the chief criterion suggested by lifeboat ethicists for determining this selective allocation of food is the population control factor—a "criterion" the moral bankruptcy of which now should be clearly evident.

My chief concern, then, comes at the point of extrapolating this "selective triage" concept from its medical context into the realm of politics and public policy. On the basis of the rather extensive reasons cited I believe that this application is inaccurate and unjustifiable. Furthermore, I believe the word "triage" presents enormous conceptual difficulties. The term contains disturbing undertones and connotations—disturbing at least when applied to human situations of emergency care and relief—of sorting according to "quality" and " the worst grade."

To the casual observer triage as it occurs in medicine and in the proposals now being referred to as "social triage," in relation to famine and other extended disasters, might at first sight seem to be one and the same thing. They may not, however, even be analogous; they certainly are not identical.

"Medical triage" implies an essentially limited selective procedure with consequences which are relatively immediate and often foreseeable. It is an interim emergency policy of short duration and limited use designed to allocate on a need basis medical and other services and supplies temporarily in short supply in order to save the lives of threatened people. Its central purpose is and always has been to save lives to the maximum possible extent.

What we are beginning to do with "social triage," as I see it, is to say: "Let's not get involved! Let's not concern ourselves—let alone inconvenience ourselves—with the problems of other peoples and nations." The scope of that concern and of our reaction to it has now reached those directly affected. Only recently Indian hunger demonstrators in Delhi carried placards which read: "Hungry people are human, too!" and, "Is India to be thrown on the rubbish heap?"[23] These are telling statements which reveal beyond any doubt that certain opinions expressed in affluent western countries in recent years, whatever their motives, have caused suspicion, fear, and indignation in the hearts of the people of India and will in due course have similar effects upon other peoples and nations as well.

In a world plagued with famine we are talking about whole populations—indeed, entire nations—who are in grave danger of death from starvation and related nutritional deficiencies. The consequences here are long-range and wholly unpredictable. In this kind of situation there is always, I believe, an implicit and significant moral danger of elevating the case-by-case evaluation (which is the essential basis of medical triage) into a legal or otherwise binding public policy regarding life and death. (The danger is similar to that which exists, for example, in adopting either of the two possible extreme positions on abortion and euthanasia and elevating these into the force of law.)

"Social triage" is by its very nature more open to corruption of objectives. There are, unhappily, a whole multiplicity of hidden objectives and alternatives (for example, politics, economics, and a variety of nationalistic or egoistic priorities) which may motivate triage to be accepted as a reasonable and logical social policy (as revealed, for example, in the recent U. S. involvement with the Chilean coup[24]). Countries which embrace "social triage" might be accused, for example, of political opportunism—of hoping that governments under the stress of famine might fall or that animosity might arise between neighboring countries to the end that situations and governments more favorable to their own might be established. We could be accused, that is to say, of neo-colonialism of the most abhorrent variety.

Nonsense, perhaps? But western governments have stood accused in the world's eyes of similar self-serving interests on far less evidence and with less justification. Experiences as a teacher in the international field of Public Health have included accusations of racism and neo-colonialism, leveled by third world representatives, for advancing what were considered medically, socially, and humanitarianly motivated proposals about methods to assist in establishing a program of population control. It is not then all that nonsensical to suggest that similar ideas might cross people's minds concerning our advocacy of "social triage" as a solution to world famine.

Ulterior motives *are* possible and these are very real and present dangers in the advocacy of "social triage." In medicine by contrast—even under full wartime conditions—the prime objective and directive of a "triage policy" is abundantly clear: it is to preserve life with the maximum efficiency with whatever facilities and resources are available.

Because medical triage is a practice which for the most part is "tried and true" and justifiable, we can use this concept in the social sphere to give the impression that we are likewise performing a humanitarian act. The medical and social situations, however, are subtly but fundamentally different. In medical triage value judgments are not normally made in dispensing aid—such as evaluating a person's present or future worth to society, his or her relative "goodness," or any other such judgment—save whether benefit can be had from the treatment we have to offer. Yet such value judgments are proposed as the central criteria for making decisions in the context of "social triage."

"Triage" in its medical context thus cannot be carried over and used as a justification for *not* providing aid to the victims of famine. We cannot take the good feelings and the sense of fairness—the justification on a case-by-case basis which is associated with medical triage—out into the world and give the impression that we have solved the problems of scarcity and just allocation in this way.

My plea, therefore, is to avoid the use of this word and this concept in the case of famine or other similar global disasters of long-range, and unpredictable consequence. "Social triage" is, I contend, a misnomer—a term which is confusing and ambiguous. This is not merely an issue of semantics, but rather one of co-opting a concept out of context to solve totally different problems. The danger in such tactics, always implicit, is that once we have convinced ourselves that a problem is solved and that we are doing what is right—no matter how wrong we may in fact be—we become capable of all manner of monstrosities in the name of justice and morality.

Some years ago, two young women were discussing how one of them would put her pet dog "to sleep" in order to be free to take her vacation later in the year. Without wishing to seem overly sentimental I would contend that the true meaning of this benign little euphemism is well known. But the effect of its use is to permit statements and behavior that otherwise would seem monstrous. If the one woman had confessed to planning the murder of her dog for the sake of her own convenience, the moral force of such words might have caused her to reexamine her position. As it was, she was *insulated* from the moral implications of her actions through *language*. Such is the power and the danger of language—and this is my reason for wishing to avoid the use of the word and concept "triage" as applied to world famine. My fear is that its use in this new context may permit us to become insulated from the horrors of famine, to abandon the search for alternative, more humane solutions to the problem, and instead comfortably to commit acts that otherwise would seem monstrous and unjust.

Roger Ascham (1515–1568), one of the great pedagogues and humanist scholars in English history, was writing tutor to Henry VIII and his children. Later he was Latin Secretary to Queen Mary I and to Queen Elizabeth I. He observed in a posthumous publication entitled *The Scholemaster*:

> He that will write well in any tongue must follow this counsel of Aristotle, to speak as the common people do, to think as wise men do. And so shall every man understand him, and the judgment of wise men laud him.[25]

As we join together in the search for a just solution to the problem of feeding the world's hungry, let us likewise follow this counsel. Let us speak with plain words and employ clear concepts. Thus may we understand our problems fully and face them with courage, justice, and mercy.

As we look back over the last seventy-five years with two world wars, with the development, perfection, and threat of nuclear weapons (now no longer a monopoly of the western world) and a wide range of sophisticated weapons of war in armories all over the world, with people and nations jostling one another for the dwindling supplies of fossil fuels and other commodities, with doubt, deceit, and suspicion ever mounting to hatred to divide nations into camps, the words of Sidney Webb (1859–1947), written in the first year of the twentieth century, come echoing across the years to serve as one further warning.

> We have become aware almost in a flash that we are not merely individuals, but members of a community nay citizens of the world . . . In short, the opening of the 20th century finds us all, to the dismay of the old-fashioned individualist, thinking in communities.[26]

At the World Food Conference held in Rome in November 1974 Henry Kissinger reiterated Sidney Webb's prophetic statement to remind us once again that we are all people of one world, ever growing smaller.

> Once famine was considered part of the normal cycle of man's existence, a local or at worst a national tragedy. Now our consciousness is global. Our achievements, our expectations, and our moral convictions have made this issue into a universal political concern.[27]

Persons and nations cannot live merely for the sake of their survival alone. The time has come at last when, pressured by the forces of nature and history, we must learn to live for one another.

NOTES

1. Thomas R. Malthus, *An Essay* (London: 1826).
2. F. Darwin, *The Life and Letters of Charles Darwin*, 3 vols. (London: 1887).
3. "Man's Population Predicament," *Population Bulletin*, vol. 26, No. 2 (Washington, D. C.: The Population Reference Bureau, Inc., 1972).
4. P. M. Hauser, "Population of the World," *Study of Population and Immigration Problems* (Washington, D. C.: U. S. Government Printing Office, 1962).
5. *The Compact Edition of the Oxford English Dictionary* (London: Oxford University Press, 1971).

6. *Webster's Third New International Dictionary*, 15th ed. (Springfield, Mass.: Merriam, 1966).
7. *Dorland's Illustrated Medical Dictionary*, 25th ed. (Philadelphia: W. B. Saunders, 1965); *Blakiston's New Gould's Medical Dictionary*, 2nd ed. (New York; McGraw-Hill, 1956); and *Stedman's Medical Dictionary*, 22nd ed. (Baltimore: Williams & Wilkins, 1972).
8. *The British Medical Dictionary*, edited by Sir Arthur MacNalty Caston (London and New York, 1971).
9. *Stedman's Medical Dictionary*.
10. *The Surgical Memoirs of Baron Larrey*, Vols. I and II trans. by R. W. Hall; Vol. III trans. by J. C. Mercer (1812–1818).
11. *The Military Surgeon*, Vols. 23–115 (1908–1954).
12. *Journal of Military Medicine*, Vols. 116–140 (1955–75).
13. (London: H. M. S. O., 1952–1972).
14. *Activities of Surgical Consultants*, Vol. II of *Surgery in World War II* (Washington, D. C.: Office of the Surgeon General, Dept. of the Army, 1962).
15. Ibid.
16. Henry Beecher, *Research and the Individual* (Boston: Little, Brown, and Co., 1971), p. 209–10.
17. In addition to some of the references to population cited above see also: E. A. Wrigley, *Population and History* (New York: World University Library, 1969); Behrman, Corsa and Freedman (eds.) *Fertility and Family Planning: A World View* (Ann Arbor: University of Michigan Press, 1970; Lester R. Brown, *In the Human Interest* (New York: W. W. Norton & Co., 1974); Daniel Callahan (ed.), *The American Population Debate* (New York: Anchor Books, 1971).
18. John Boyd-Orr, *The White Man's Dilemma* (New York: British Book Center, 1948).
19. Daniel Defoe, *Tour Thro the Whole Island of Great Britain*, 3 Vols. (1724–1726).
20. William Cobbett, *Rural Rides* (1821).
21. Stuart W. Hinds, "Difficulties Experienced by Schools of Public Health in Europe Meeting the Needs of the Newly Developing Countries," *Symposium on Schools of Public Health*, edited by S. W. Hinds (Rennes, France: World Health Organization, 1965), EURO 304.
22. R. E. Miles, *Population Bulletin*, Vol. 27, No. 1 (1971).
23. N. Cousins, "Peril Seen in Ignoring the Hungry," *Houston Post* (Feb. 15, 1975).
24. Cf. G. R. Lucas, Jr., "Famine and Global Policy: An Interview with Joseph Fletcher," *Christian Century* (Sept. 3–10, 1975), 755.
25. Roger Ascham, *The Scholemaster* (1570).
26. J. M. MacKintosh, *Topics in Public Health* (London: Livingston, 1965).
27. Henry A. Kissinger, "The Threat of Famine," *Vital Speeches of the Day*, Vol. 41 (1974), pp. 98–102.

FEEDING THE HUNGRY:
An Ethical Appraisal

JOSEPH FLETCHER

W HAT MIGHT BE MORALLY RIGHT to do in some situations could be wrong in other situations. This is the relativity of ethics. The specific down-to-earth question at stake in this inquiry is whether we ought to feed the starving in places like Bangladesh and the Sahel of sub-Sahara Africa.

I would hate to think that the virtue of generosity has gone out of style. There is certainly no hard evidence that it has, in spite of charges frequently brought by romanticists against the "modern world" and the "new morality." Like most of the classic virtues, however, generosity is two-faced and double-edged; not only is it truly virtuous but it makes us *feel* good and makes us feel we *are* good. It is like being proud of being humble. The virtues are heady stuff; they can become addictive, and once hooked, we practice them without critical restraint.

Opinions about the workability and desirability of famine relief are remarkably diverse. Politicians and churchmen call upon their constituents to give generously to programs of varying sizes and efficiency, aimed at feeding the starving in teeming underdeveloped countries. Yet a bishop recently gave open expression to the doubts which functionaries of his kind usually paper over with moralistic appeals, by saying that as a condition of aid "vasectomies should go along with the groceries."

Author of the well-known *Situation Ethics* (Westminster, 1966), Mr. Fletcher has in recent years given special attention to ethical problems in biomedical fields. Formerly Professor of Social Ethics at the Episcopal Theological School (Cambridge, Mass.), he is currently serving a dual appointment as Visiting Professor of Medical Ethics at the University of Virginia School of Medicine (Charlottesville), and at the Institute of Religion and Human Development (Texas Medical Center, Houston, Texas).

The hardcore question here has to do with the equation between starvation and uncontrolled human fertility. In any economy if demand (the number of people to be fed) exceeds supply (the amount of food they produce), prices (reflected in malnutrition and starvation) will increase. Intervention by famine relief from outside (like wage and price controls in the free market) may ameliorate the condition but the trouble remains nonetheless.

Although the problem is simple logically, it can be quite complex existentially. There are many variables in the arithmetic of population, land, food yield, and weather, so that moral concern without demographers and geographers to undergird and inform it cannot be trusted to reach sound judgments as to where and when food relief actually will or will not help. The data of these specialists are decisive if we want to tailor our ethical analyses to real situations. Ethically regarded, moral judgments or normative decisions are no better than their facts.

To speak seriously of whether relief will help or will not help comes as a shock to the more innocent advocates of generosity. These innocents are the ones whom cynics like to dismiss as do-gooders. Idealists have even been known to say they would rather die than go on living in a world where decisions to survive are made at the price of millions of lives. They say this with equally lofty sentiment both about using thermonuclear weapons and letting people starve when they could be fed. They refuse ever to "think the unthinkable," preferring to cry *Fiat justitia, pereat mundus*—"let justice be done even if the world perish."

I believe we have to accept and respect a sacrificial ethics. To prefer death itself rather than survive selfishly is an honorable choice. But this is the case only as long as such choices are made within the ambit of personal and interpersonal relations. Voluntarily to choose suicide or to enter into a suicide pact is defensible ethically. In social relations, however, it is another story. Any realistic appraisal of our human condition will show that group egos (biological species, families, ethnic groups, nation states) simply do not choose to die. Sacrificial altruism is never an option, except in the case of individuals making the choice for themselves. Imposing a choice of pain or death on one's neighbors and fellows is ethically of an altogether different order.

It does not follow that simply because men cling to survival it is therefore the right thing to do. What is is not *ipso facto* what ought to be. Nevertheless, most of us are convinced that survival is not only a biological imperative but that it makes very good sense ethically as well. I agree with Hans Jonas, for example, that corporate survival for mankind is the highest good, the *summum bonum*, for the ultimate and simple reason that without survival no other values have any meaning.[1] In these terms there is a good case to be made for the "tyranny of survival."[2]

LIMITING PRINCIPLES

We must presuppose that no responsible person would insist on sharing regardless of the consequences, whether in matters of food or anything else. Such a posture would be purblind and irrational. We ought not to enter upon courses of action which foreseeably end in the negation of the good being sought. If it could be shown that the beneficiaries of our generosity would, on balance, suffer more than they benefitted, and if it is our proper business as moral agents to optimize the good, rather than blindly following a moral rule or value (virtue), then in such a situation to share the food would be immoral. We should give if it helps but not if it hurts. This reasoning has the most direct bearing on many problems of famine relief. It simply is not always true that it is "more blessed to give than to receive."

Catholic priests in proverty-stricken areas of Latin America, for example, do not interfere with the public health nurses and midwives who are teaching women how to use contraceptives, even though the clergy are committed by church authority to the ethical rule that artificial birth control is immoral. They turn a blind eye because they reason consequentially: this is the way to reduce both abortions and the flow of unwanted babies. They forsake their moral rule, flouting the virtue of obedience, for the sake of the greater good.

Could it not be, then, that in some situations in the world the virtue of generosity—in the form of food relief—should be set aside? Are there not places where food relief would result in keeping the starving alive long enough to procreate even more people to starve, without closing the gap between their production of food and their production of hungry bellies—in effect only adding to the numbers of those who die of disease and starvation? For each one individually, food might solve the problem, but for the country socially it only makes things worse. It increases the spread of disease and starvation and death.

Death statistics if kept at all would read "flu" and "stomach trouble" and "heart failure," but the deaths thus recorded would in truth be a function of malnutrition and starvation. Irrational compassion says "Give them food," but rational compassion says "No." Alan Gregg, a past vice-president of the Rockefeller Foundation, used to say that overpopulation is a cancer and that he'd never heard of a cancer being cured by feeding it.[3]

Alan Berg of the World Bank, a very gung-ho advocate of feeding the starving, admits reluctantly that it is only an "assumption" that food supplies "over a long enough (sic) period" will allow at least a low-nutrition diet in some countries.[4] This assumption is itself based on another, namely, "on the assumption that population growth can somehow (sic) be brought under control in low-income countries." But what, we must ask, is the price in terms of human misery and death which will have to be paid for this indeterminate period during which additional millions of human beings are born, suffer, and die? Berg says, "If it were not for aid, there would be many more starving babies." In flat contradiction I have to insist that *because* of aid there will be *more* starving babies.

In trying to optimize the good—to do as much good as we can—it is necessary to make cost-benefit analyses and trade-off judgments. We must have as much data as we can get about everybody involved, with their different needs and potentials, using the guideline of proportionate good (cost-benefit) and choosing between competing values (trade-offs). As a matter of fact, this ethical methodology applies across the board from famine relief on the big scale to offers of food to individual panhandlers on the street. Looked at ethically, the question is whether we are obliged in conscience to feed those who are hungry if to do so in a given situation decreases the sum of human wellbeing, and like any sensible and sensitive almsgiver, I answer in the negative.

We have two questions to cope with, however, not merely one. (1) *When should we not share at all?*, and (2) *When should we share, on what conditions, and how much?* The first one is the problem of reverse effect or self-defeating generosity, and the second deals with allocation, "social triage," or distributive justice.[5] These questions in recent times have been examined and analyzed most significantly by Garrett Hardin.[6]

HARDIN'S LIFEBOAT ETHICS

Hardin's thesis is based on the premise that there are limits to growth. Like John Stuart Mill he recognizes that the generosity of charitable men can and probably will cut across or even undermine the general welfare. He contends that U. S. food resources are in fact far less plentiful than is commonly supposed. He estimates that this country today has only a 37–day grace period against chronic food shortages as compared to 238 days in 1962. The worldwide phenomenon of double-digit inflation in part reflects the dependence of the standard of living in national economies on the functional ratio between labor productivity, soil conditions, crop yield, and weather norms.

There are indeed limits to growth, and we face not only prospective shortages in many things but palpable limitations as a present fact in such essential items as energy (especially fossil fuels) and food. Jay Forrester and others, with different models, have variously calculated and computerized the breakdown point globally and nationally in the balance of the five basic factors—population, pollution, raw materials, food supply, and industrial output. They all find it within decades, not centuries. Therefore, Hardin's argument runs, we must husband our resources and calculate their consumption carefully.

For several years now Hardin has been warning us as a social biologist that the selfish and rapacious will victimize everybody else in a given system if the system is based on unrestricted individual consumption of resources held in common. This process he calls "the tragedy of the commons."[7] He cites as his model the history of common grazing lands.

He reasons that because of individual greed, reinforced by the feeling "If I don't take it somebody else will, and why not me?" the system will break down and the majority will suffer unless participation is held down to a *quid pro quo* basis. The Christian and Marxist ultimate ideals of the Kingdom of God and communism are not workable unless everybody is either willing or compelled to abide by a distributively just allocation. Therefore, as far as food goes, the chronically hungry will sooner or later enhunger the rest of the world. "The fundamental error of the sharing ethic is," he says, "that it leads to the tragedy of the commons."

It seems to me that Hardin's error is overstatement. His propositions are not sufficiently modified. He should say, more carefully, "The fundamental error of the sharing ethic is that it leads to the tragedy of the commons *if it is practiced without critical limits.*" The true thrust of his reasoning is *not* to repudiate sharing, but to insist that it be paired with responsibility. Beneficiaries are required to use the help they receive in an optimal fashion, thus permitting the benefactors foreseeably to "get off the hook." An obvious inference is that countries suffering from chronic famine should control their fertility in return for food relief. This limiting principle follows the line of a model familiar to biologists, based on the "reciprocal altruism" they observe in certain species of mammalian and submammalian animals.[8]

To many of his readers and hearers Hardin seems to have developed his thesis as if it applies *without exception* to any country which will not or cannot accept reciprocal conditions for food relief. If this is a misunderstanding of his "lifeboat ethics," it is as much due to his failure to say so plainly as it is to the angry feelings loosed against him by his simplistically open-handed opponents. He owes it to us all to address himself more exactly to the question of *when* his principle of "mutual coercion mutually agreed upon" may be disregarded. He ought to explain, as he has as yet not explained, just when and how far sharing with the hungry becomes "counterproductive."

As it stands now, Hardin's thesis appears to be unacceptably doctrinaire and universalistic, a case of a principle becoming his prison. I hasten to say, however, that he is no more imprisoned by principle than are his sentimental critics, who dismiss him as a hardhearted Ebenezer Scrooge. (No *ad hominem* characterization could in actual fact be farther from the truth, as his whole life pattern has made abundantly plain.)

I would not be as hardnosed, then, as Hardin seems to be. I am willing to share food with the undisciplined and the undeserving—even with the apparently unredeemable panhandlers of this world—whether they be individual persons or whole nations. However, *there are two situations in which it is ethically correct to draw the line: (1) When the probable consequences of sharing would endanger the survival of the majority whose interests are involved, givers as well as receivers*, and (2) *When the probable consequences of sharing would increase rather than relieve the recipients' misery*. These two situations, separately or together, are good and sufficient reason to "let 'em starve."

After all, Hardin is not saying "Let's never share our food." His concern is that we should not *waste* whatever food is available for sharing. Furthermore, beyond the question of optimal benefits in relief, he sees clearly that in some situations *more* people will die of disease and starvation if we give them food that keeps them alive long enough to reproduce more hungry offspring. This is *a net loss of human lives* rather than a net gain, exacerbating rather than relieving human suffering. As both a humanitarian and a utilitarian, Hardin cannot in good conscience support famine relief in such situations; like the rest of us, he is committed to human life as a first-order value, and believes our ethical task is to serve that good.

WHEN NOT TO SHARE

Of the two questions calling for a fresh hard look (the first being when not to share at all and the second when to share but on what conditions and how much), I want to examine the first one more sharply and rigorously than has Hardin. I want to contend that the first question is a fairly simple one. Even though we *can* feed the starving in places like Bangladesh and Niger we ought not to do it—presuming that they will not be able to limit their reproduction for quite a while because of cultural taboos and reproductive mores.

Food sharing in such situations is what I have called elsewhere the "capacity fallacy"—the notion that we ought to share something because we can.[9] It does not follow that because we can we should. To go directly from "is" to "ought" is ethical foolishness. This is certainly the case when it increases human misery or hurts more people than ever. If by feeding starving people we enable them to procreate more starvers, only in turn to die of nutritional diseases and starvation, mankind will have been hurt—not helped.

In Bangladesh, already with 1400 people per square mile, seven babies are born every minute. For millions of parents, these children are thought to be their only security, if and when the children manage to grow up. If only two out of five manage somehow to survive, they will have doomed three of their own children in order to better their own chance of not dying. It is a parlay *en masse*, using human lives as chips—a gambling game of life and death heavily reinforced by religious teaching. Individual procreators, looking to their personal gain and "security," victimized their own children individually and their fellow countrymen collectively, as well as any foreign donors who send them food.

As late as the eighteenth century in England people had several children in order that a few might survive the high infant mortality. There was enough food to go around. For example, John Stuart Mill's grandfather, James, gave his name to three baby boys, hoping that at least one bearing the name would live to manhood; only one did. But their problem was due to infant mortality and a lack of medical know-how, not to famine.

In the Sahel children would die of malnutrition even if they had the best medical care (they do not). The problem of overpopulation in such places will not necessarily be solved by withholding food relief; such a measure would certainly not in and by itself solve the problem. Nevertheless it would at least not compound the problem. The onus of multiplying empty stomachs in the Sahel lies exactly where it belongs, on a callous progenitive populace.

Whenever it can be shown that certain countries have exceeded their biological carrying capacity, yet will not or cannot achieve a stationary state in population growth (to say nothing of reversing it), then to give them food is immoral. The wealth or poverty of potential donors is ethically irrelevant. Giving aid in such situations could be defended only in or by an ethics which allows its moral agents to follow principles regardless of the consequences.

Those who protest against Hardin's "lifeboat" analogy because of the wealth in America—portraying our economy as much more like a luxury yacht—are certainly correct up to a point. There is no real comparison between our affluence and the niggardly resources of underdeveloped countries. This difference could conceivably have a bearing on how far we can go in sharing before it becomes unfair to *us*, the giver. But it is irrelevant so far as the recipients are concerned in those counterproductive situations where sharing *increases* the number of human beings who suffer and die.

We are dealing here with a false dilemma, because the imperative of generosity becomes irrational. Conflicted consciences exist only because of the guilt *feelings*, not guilt, which arise if we refuse food to the hungry. To feed and *be* guilty or not to feed and *feel* guilty—that is the question. It is much like Michael Tooley's Diabolical Machine.[10] John and Mary are in a machine. If you push a button John dies; if you don't, Mary dies. Somebody dies either way, and you cannot avoid choosing by not choosing. The foreseeable consequence is death, for John or Mary. But the dilemma ceases to be so stark once you ask the question of social ethics: which way offers the most good (or least harm) for the most people? If "John" represents a given number of lives but "Mary" more, you push the button. The significant differential is utility. Which way depends on that criterion—preponderant benefit. It means that feeding the hungry is sometimes wrong.

None of this, of course, offers any excuse for refusing to help such hapless peoples in other ways. They can be helped in a fundamental fashion with accumulation of capital, technical advice and training, education, medical care (especially fertility control), and soil fertilization and cycling. Indeed, this is the only *constructive* way to share, even though in some cases of underdevelopment (but certainly not in all) it might be right also to send some food relief. The biggest difference between rich and poor countries, after all, is not in the food they consume but in the energy they use. People in rich lands get less than twice as many calories as the poor and only three times as much protein. But they have ten times as much energy to use by reason of their developed tools of production—technologies amplifying the output per unit of human labor.

As the Chinese proverb says, "Give a man a fish and he eats for a day; teach him to fish and he eats all his life" (or at least as long as there are any fish left to catch!). This is why a certain American private foundation, religiously motivated, recently gave $375,000 for a pilot irrigation project in Niger, but not a cent for food. Making fishermen is true generosity; doling out fish to the fishless is at best unconstructive and at worst unethical.

OBJECTIONS TO NOT SHARING

Roger Revelle of the Harvard Center for Population Studies has gone so far as to call Hardin's thesis "obscene" (an indication of the deep emotion aroused), even though he agrees that population control is the key to the problem.[11] His contention, however, is that the only way to reduce and control populations is to provide the technical assistance needed to raise the gross national product (GNP) of the underdeveloped and starving countries. A higher GNP results in an increase of capital instruments, which increases the productivity of human labor. Furthermore, the argument goes, this increased productivity is always (sic) accompanied by a corresponding *decrease* in fertility and therefore of population pressure.

This "demographic transition" theory does not hold very much water; it is probably a "wishful thinking" theory. And its nutritional version is sheer nonsense—that is, the old "Brazilian thesis" that technical development and higher income lead to better nutrition, especially protein consumption, and that proteins cause fecundity to drop: in short, higher protein equals lower fecundity.[12] Both biologically and historically the theory breaks down. A higher standard of living does not necessarily nor invariably result in a lower birth rate.

The fact is that in many countries, for example even in Ireland and France, a rising GNP has been dogged step by step by a rising population. Runaway population growth ("explosion") is entirely a modern phenomenon, only in effect since the capital development of the world; until about 300 years ago the world's population growth had a rate of less than a thousandth of one percent, but with a rising GNP it has reached a two percent per annum growth rate. This is the whole story of the United States; a tremendous technical development paired with a tremendous population growth. Only in the Big Depression of the Twenties and Thirties did family size decline—although, as at present, births have declined for varying periods in the general upward trend.

Food relief advocates appeal to our *amour propre*, claiming that we will be looked upon as moral lepers if we do not send food to countries like Senegal. On its own merits alone this is a particularly cynical line to take. Basing our actions on a "public relations" appeal to image-making (ethical analysis pushed back to the jump seat) would turn our inquiry into a absurd non-solution for a non-problem. A quite different and more arresting objection is that the consequence of saying "No!" to those in great distress would be self-brutalization, hardening our hearts and making for callous consciences. How are we to weigh moralistic accusations in the scales against the logic of a humanitarian ethics?

Perhaps the strangest argument for giving food in spite of predictably fatal effects is that the relief given would not have a significant impact anyway, due to political corruption, logistics, storage, and epidemic disease. The argument is, essentially, "Don't worry about increasing the number who die. Your help won't reach the starving anyway." This point was actually made to me in discussion, as a support argument for giving aid to "keep up our image in the eyes of the world."Obviously, if this were true it would be wrong to send food uselessly to a sub-marginal land when other places need it for constructive growth.

In Hardin's terminology we can say that in *some* situations (but *only* some, not all), to feed the hungry is not "melioristic" (making things better) but actually "pejoristic" (making things worse). As applied to the problem of when to feed the hungry, I myself prefer to say that we should offer the hungry true help, but not "self-defeating sharing" or "negative relief." In such cases I favor instead a policy of "benign neglect," a phrase coined in another context several years ago by Patrick Moynihan, now America's ambassador to the United Nations.

Contributors to the discussion sometimes appeal to the "right" of the hungry to be fed. This is a rather superficial and uncritical brand of moral rhetoric. Rights or moral claims are at best only relatively valid. Moral philosophers and casuists point to problems of "perplexity" where two or more supposed rights conflict with one another in practice. Jurisprudence and law deal constantly with conflicts of rights.

Our specific question is whether the people of certain countries have a valid claim on others for aid (a right) if giving them food would cause more people to be born and suffer and die than are already caught up in such miseries. The most appalling instance of an irrational appeal to rights surfaced at the 1973 World Congress on Population in Romania in speeches by spokesmen for "the third world." They kept saying, in effect, "We have a right to be fed to keep from dying, but nobody has a right to ask us to limit our babymaking."

There is a widespread "feeling" that everybody has a "god-given right" to produce at will; therefore to suggest any rational conditions for its exercise sets our cerebral and visceral functions at war with each other. The resulting discomfort gives rise to some high-flown but sentimental principles; one such is, "We ought to feed the hungry just because they are hungry." An FAO economist recently exemplified this posture in a nearly perfect *petitio principii* or pattern of circular thinking. Discussing the problem of feeding starving nations, he said, "It shall be done because it must be done."[13] This kind of talk is the bankruptcy of human reason. Logic aside, however, the issue as a whole shows how policy choices hang on differences in ethics.

WHEN SHOULD WE SHARE?

So much for the question "When should we not share food at all?" Now for the second of our basic questions: "When *should* we share—on what conditions, and how much?"

When should we help? Given compassion and a concern for human values, we ought to share when there is need. In any humanistic ethic, whether religiously sanctioned or not, human need is a claim on those who can help. As we have said, however, this claim is not universally or absolutely valid. And what are the conditions for helping? Surely a sound guideline is reponsibility. Responsibility would be a willingness on the receiver's part, expressed in an agreement and in subsequent practice, to turn the giver's largesse into the fullest effect with the quickest endpoint possible.

In those countries where famine occurs not as an unexpected misfortune but as a consequence of population exceeding environmental carrying capacity, responsibility calls for the achievement of a balance between production and reproduction on some agreed time scale. The projected rate of progress must at least be speedy enough to avoid the self-defeating generosity caused by an unethical reproduction level—a point already discussed. The balance may not have to be struck at once and hardly ever could be, but the commitment to it and the evidence of its realizability should be crucial.

Using Hardin's formula, responsible dealings depend upon mutual coercion mutually agreed upon. As John Rawls likes to maintain, there is no justice without fairness; conscientious sharing requires, as he puts it, "principles that free and rational persons concerned to further their own interests would accept in an initial position . . . to regulate all further agreements."[14]

Finally, then, we face the question of *how much*. How much are we obliged in good conscience to give? In classical rhetoric this is the question of distributive justice. If the survival of the human species is the highest good to which all other values are relative (as we have postulated), it is logically necessary to consider all food relief proposals within the context of the *total* food resources available, to both the donor(s) and recipient(s). What should go to the beneficiary(ies) should therefore be expressed in a percentage of what is available to the benefactor. This form of reasoning holds even when we assume that our humanitarian motive (the virtue of generosity) will cause us to make that percentage as big as we possibly can.

On a foundation of hard numbers data we can then turn to *three crucially important questions*. The absence of these questions in Hardin's exposition should cause us to be less than satisfied with his treatment of the problem. The three questions are: When does it hurt to help? When is it dangerous to help? When is it suicidal—self-destructive—to help?

The figure below is a graphic presentation of the problem. The gradient 0 (for zero) to Y is the curve of famine relief known to be possible; the vector 0 to A is the total amount of food available to the donor (in quintals of grain or dollars); the vector 0 to B is the amount actually given in relief; and the coordinates are the points at which relief would hurt (X_1), then endanger (X_2), and finally destroy the doner (X_3).

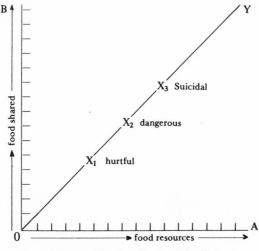

Figure: Sharing food ethically.

Not being competent as a moral philosopher to make even a rough guess as to where these cutoff points would come in hard numbers on the sharing curve, I can only call upon the demographers, geographers, and others for their input. But what we need are not just data; we need knowledgeable calculations to indicate where these sequential points of decision should fall. These calculations are requred if we are to engage in the morally serious business of (a) saving human lives and (b) raising the quality of these lives.

Sharing out of so much affluence that the donor "never even feels it" can be a form of cheap grace. The very rich, the well off, and the modestly comfortable, all alike, should be ready to share when responsible reciprocal conditions have been honored. There are, of course, a number of variables in the three parameters—hurt, danger, and self-destruct—due to differing values, styles of life, economic and political systems. Yet I for one would contend that a humane ethics calls for more than cheap grace; that when we share we ought to do it even if it hurts. On the sharing curve it is not too much to say that we ought to give until it hurts.

By hurting I mean, of course, the donor's hurt. In the forum of conscience we may as sharers hurt ourselves but not others, unless it be in order to help them by means of hurting them. (This would not be the case if we tried to feed countries caught in the circular futility of chronic famine.) But we should share our wealth to help a country develop out of poverty and mere subsistence. Such *felt* generosity could take the form of increasing the efficiency of our use of fuel and energy (as in automobiles and furnaces), returning to range instead of grain-fed beef (steers are notoriously wasteful as a way to convert proteins), support for a substantial U. S. contribution to the World Bank's funds to help underdeveloped countries, even personalized contributions to aid funds raised as in OXFAM—America's program of "fasts" on 600 college campuses, the students contributing the money saved thereby.

There are both public (governmental) and private ways to share instead of hogging. But let us be quite clear that to be ethical *such help to the hurt-point must be for developmental assistance, with food aid going only to emergency famine relief* (e.g., victims of sudden typhoons and earthquakes), *not to chronic famine relief*. A distinction is coming into use between Third World countries where population has not exceeded carrying capacity, thus allowing for growth and development, and Fourth World countries which obliterate all the gains made by and with them under the flood of human fertility. To help the people in such countries is morally wrong.

It would be foolish and arbitrary to say how far we ought to go past "hurt" toward endangering our own survival. We need actual cases, plus the relevant data, to see how the sharing works out—and what we decide in one case might not fit another. Yet occasionally we might as communities and nations even go beyond hurting to the danger point. There are times when we take substantial risks out of compassion or fraternal concern, as when we enter wars to help nations unjustly aggressed against, even though defeat might be the end result, or when we dive in to help a swimmer in trouble. *Unreasonable risk* means courting the ultimate disaster, nonsurvival. Since we have already determined that no country or national economy will or should knowingly commit suicide, the ultimate cutoff point on sharing would therefore seem to be unreasonable risk—which falls somewhere on the gradient between dangerous sharing and suicidal sharing. That point in every relief program will have to be established situationally.

Still thinking in generalized terms, we can say that sharing short of danger is clearly virtuous if and when what is given is responsibly received. Ethically, this stance favors average or "aggregate" utility (human happiness) rather than "total."[15] The difference is between, for example, aiming at a million moderately well fed people (aggregate) or 500 thousand fully or maximally fed people (total). Sharing entails being willing to forego the maximum for the sake of the minimum, what is best for the greatest number, stopping short only of the minimum required for survival.

Conclusions

The reasoning we have followed brings us to four global policy propositions about moral responses to famine. They may be expressed as moral imperatives, "oughts," or obligations. Two are positive, two are negative.

(1) *Positive.* We ought to share with the starving until it hurts; conceivably we ought to share beyond that, yet short of unreasonable risk. All of this, however, should be on a basis of

contractual assistance or of "mutual coercion mutually agreed upon." We ought to share for the sake of the recipients' immediate wellbeing, our own interest entering consideration as just one of the remote consequences. We should distinguish between *food* aid and constructive assistance—things like capital equipment, education, health care, fertilizer, and technical advice. Those who give food without any strings attached simply because people are starving and without first studying the consequences obviously do not not care primarily about saving human lives; they choose to use human beings as pawns in some other game—power politics, "relief rackets," or image making.

(2) *Positive.* In our own minds we must emphasize and aim at prevention rather than rescue or crisis intervention. An analogy is to be found in medicine, which the simple-minded conceive as crisis treatment instead of preventive care. Crises occur, of course, and have to be dealt with. But in developing solutions for mass hunger, avoidance before the fact of misery is more "virtuous" than simple generosity after the fact.

(3) *Negative.* We ought to oppose the merely political use of food, just as we ought to oppose its manipulation by sentimental and/or professional relief programmers. Political food relief is "the name of the game" in U. S. Public Law 480, established as a "Food for Peace" program. Primarily it is a tool of those who administer foreign affairs (State Department and Pentagon). At present they use food surpluses to gain strategic advantages along what they call America's "defense perimeter." For example, one half of the food in our stocks available to help the hungry in 1973 went to Cambodia and Vietnam; out of the whole world of backward or developing countries where very real hunger existed, half of all we had went to those two minute and only marginally-needy lands.

When President Allende of Chile asked for wheat and offered to pay cash he was turned down flat, but when a military junta killed him and took control of the country, our officials offered them *on credit* eight times as much as Allende had asked. We need to know more than we do about what is going on in Food for Peace, the Agency for International Development, the Bank of International Settlements, and any other channels of food relief.[16]

(4) *Negative.* We ought to have an international food bank, rather than carry out our help unilaterally or even bilaterally.

The Soviet Union, the People's Republic of China, and the oil-rich governments of the Middle East ought to take their fair share of the burden of emergency food relief. And most important of all, this international famine relief agency should guarantee that it will put an end to any more unconditional grants of food. There ought to be no more tragedy of the commons.

No imaginable condition for giving help is as basic to a responsible policy as fertility control. It would be absurd to call on a global scale for deposits of surplus food in such a bank, to be available in crises to hungry countries, if withdrawals could be made unconditionally and without respect to *why* help is needed. As applied to a food bank the Marxist ideal of communism, "from each as he is able and to each as he has need," would be a disaster—in the long run especially for the undeveloped peoples themselves.

SUMMARY

The crux of the reasoning here is that unconditional famine relief does not alleviate human misery, it only adds to it. It is therefore an immoral practice, whether we are sharing our last crust or giving out of a full granary. If it can be shown to cause more hunger and misery, it is wrong to share. When sharing is helpful, we should give food to the starving—yet only as a stop-gap measure and only when there is a reasonable prospect of lowering the population level to the beneficiary's carrying capacity. It is vitally important to apply limiting principles to generosity. Properly understood, feeding the hungry as an act in itself is not ethical.

NOTES

1. Hans Jonas, "Technology and Responsibility: Reflections on the New Tasks of Ethics," *Social Research* 40 (1973) 31–54.
2. See Daniel Callahan, *The Tyranny of Survival* (New York: Macmillan Publishing Company, 1973), esp. ch. 4.
3. Alan Gregg, M.D., "A Medical Aspect of the Population Problem," *Science* 121 (1955) 681–82.
4. Quoted in Ward Greene, "Triage," *New York Times Sunday Magazine* (January 5, 1975), 9 ff.
5. "Triage" as a classical medical term is inappropriate to the famine relief discussion because of its restricted clinical range. It applies to a limited number of patients and the allocation of limited medical resources. Famine relief is a mass allocation problem. It remains true, of course, that triage in

the sense of selectivity or preferential treatment applies to both limited and mass allocations. Both are finite. The ethical problem is, when should preference go to those with the best chance of survival and when to those with the least chance?

6. Garrett Hardin, "Lifeboat Ethics: The Case Against Helping the Poor," 8 *Psychology Today* (1974) 38–43, 124–26; and "Living on a Lifeboat," *Bioscience* 24 (1974) 561–68.
7. Garrett Hardin, "The Tragedy of the Commons," *Science* 161 (1968) 1243–248.
8. See R. L. Trivers, "The Evolution of Reciprocal Altruism," *Quarterly Review of Biology* 46 (1971) 35–57.
9. Joseph Fletcher, *The Ethics of Genetic Control* (New York: Doubleday-Anchor, 1974) pp. 5–6.
10. In a paper read at the Atlanta, Georgia, meeting of the Eastern Division, American Philosophical Association, November, 1974.
11. Roger Revelle, "The Ghost at the Feast," *Science* 186 (1974) 9.
12. Josue de Castro, *The Geography of Hunger* (Boston: Little Brown, 1952).
13. Robert C. Tetro, quoted in T. Y. Canby, "Can the World Feed Its People?" 148 *National Geographic* (1975) 31.
14. John Rawls, *A Theory of Justice* (Cambridge, Massachusetts: Harvard University Press, 1971) p. 11.
15. J. J. C. Smart, "An Outline of a System of Utilitarian Ethics," in J. J. C. Smart and Bernard Williams, *Utilitarianism: For and Against* (Cambridge, England: Cambridge University Press, 1973) pp. 27–28.
16. Some political judgments are relevant, of course. If a recipient country's regime is plainly inimical or incompetent, it ought not to be given relief without corrective agreements. To refuse merely for ideological reasons is, however, inhumane and therefore wrong.

INDIVIDUALS AND COMMUNITIES, PRESENT AND FUTURE:
Towards a Morality in a Time of Famine

H. TRISTRAM ENGELHARDT, JR.

T HE CONCEPT OF SOCIAL TRIAGE is a response to a reality (widespread and increasing famine) and a challenge to traditional humanistic attitudes (e.g., that one should feed the hungry). In part the concept of "social triage" alters the medical meaning of triage: one is not now choosing among societies on the basis of which ones have a chance to survive when the circumstances are such that not all can survive (as one chooses in medical triage to treat only those who have a chance to benefit when there is not enough time, material, personnel, etc., to treat everyone). Rather it is probably the case that at least for the short run all societies can survive if the levels of food and energy consumption in the developed countries are lowered and the difference distributed.

One is not yet asking *who* shall survive, but whether there is a moral duty for the well off to forego affluence so that *all* can survive for the short run: (1) even when populations in some societies are starving in great part due to their unchecked population growth, and (2) even when feeding them may itself accelerate population expansion (by increasing fertility) and thus enlarging the number of persons starving.[1] These issues

Mr. Engelhardt holds doctorates in both philosophy and medicine. He is Associate Professor of the Philosophy of Medicine in the Institute for the Medical Humanities and the Department of Preventive Medicine and Community Health in the University of Texas Medical Branch at Galveston. His contributions in this field will be brought together in a forthcoming book, *Medical Ethics* (In Preparation); he is also the author of *Mind-Body: A Categorial Relation*.

have recently been addressed under metaphors such as social triage or lifeboat ethics.[2]

Here I will hope to show some of the questions behind such metaphors. The conclusions I will support may in part be similar to those of Garrett Hardin's. The difference lies in the grounds for the conclusions. Since reasons reach beyond any particular conclusions, they structure the sense of our morality in a time of famine and are therefore the more important.

I. CREATING RESPONSIBILITIES FOR OTHERS:
   THE REQUIREMENT OF GOODWILL

For simplicity's sake I will not discuss whether the developed countries have special obligations to the underdeveloped in virtue of the past use of such countries through colonial or economic relationships that may have contributed unfairly to the good of the developed countries at the expense of the underdeveloped. All such issues must be resolved to understand concretely the status of claims by starving societies for food. I will make do with attempting half the answer: what obligations do members of one society have to feed members of other societies, absent any special issues of past exploitations?

By omitting mention of the history of exploitation among societies I do not mean to imply that these issues are not real or important. Rather it is because these issues are of substantial concern that it is useful to determine what claims exist antecedent to issues of exploitation. Moreover if strong moral claims in circumstances of need can be shown to exist in the absence of past exploitation, then one will have an account of such claims that is independent of disputed historical questions. Further, an understanding of the general character of claims between societies will have implications for any resolution of the kinds of issues that arise out of a history of past exploitation.

To begin to sort out the issues let us imagine an island upon which sixteen couples are shipwrecked. They have no hope for rescue and therefore decide to establish themselves without any expectation of leaving. After a careful survey of the island, they judge that the island can comfortably support a population of one hundred and sixty. For various reasons the original group of sixteen breaks into four units of two couples each, and the island is divided into four regions, each able to support forty persons. Group A decides to restrict its population growth so that there will never be more than forty A's in order to allow a comfortable lifestyle for their future generations. The B's decide to restrict their population to twenty so as to allow their descendants to enjoy affluence. The C's make no restrictions on their population growth though cognizant of the consequences. The D's, though, hold that it is morally wrong to use birth control, and reproduce as a matter of religious conviction.

Some years later there are forty A's, twenty B's, eighty C's, and ninety D's. With a population over twice that which is optimal for their part of the island, the C's and D's are forced to live on a near subsistence level, and in times of bad harvests many C's and D's die. The C's and D's then demand that the A's and B's share their food with them and that the B's cede them half their land. Again, there is no history of exploitation among any of the four groups. There is much controversy concerning who has a moral claim to what.

The C's and D's claim that the A's and B's have a duty to feed them in virtue of their all being persons. That is, the C's and D's argue that what is significant is that A's, B's, C's, and D's alike are implicitly members of a community of persons, having an equal claim to freedom and fair treatment regardless of the particular societies to which they may belong. An element of such fair treatment, the C's and D's claim, is provision of sufficient food for life. It is immoral, they argue, for some to live in affluence while others starve.

The A's and B's retort that to be a person is to live in a particular society with a particular history, and that the condition of the society of the C's and D's was brought about by their own policies. In contrast to the C's and D's the A's and B's invested energy and forethought in the development of a population policy acceptable to their own societies. As an act of charity the A's and B's offer to feed the C's and D's if and only if the C's and D's will agree to decrease their populations to a level at which further food will not be requisite.

It is useful to lay out an argument for such a position.

A's and B's would hold that one society may give food to another society if and only if the recipient society will do what is requisite not to perpetuate the need for that food because:

(1) all else being equal, entitlement to food comes from production of food; and

(2) societies as corporate enterprises may be viewed as the

producers of food within which a member may have a moral claim against the others for sufficient food and support for a dignified life as a member of that society, but there is not one single island (or world) society; and

(3) one society may give food to another society if the receiving society acts to decrease its future need for donated food (that is, as long as the receiving society is not using the members of the donating society as merely means for their gratis sustenance). The recipient's attempt to meet its own needs would be held, given this argument, to be integral to treating members of the donating society as persons, as objects of respect (the condition for there being obligations between the societies at all or for there being moral actions by their members is that those members be objects of respect; acting to undercut the basis of that respect by treating another as a means merely would be an act against morality in itself, an act not to be supported); and

(4) failure to decrease population expansion along with receiving food may increase the number of suffering individuals by increasing the population. If the A's and B's have good reason to hold that feeding the C's and D's will increase the number of persons starving, then by thus increasing the fertility of the starving society or by helping the members of the starving society to avoid or defer considering their general obligation to control their population growth, they would be acting to injure persons. (The second consideration extends this point not only to members of the population of reproductive age, but to the society as a whole.) A's and B's would under such circumstances be morally responsible for the increase in suffering due to their interventions. They would be abetting the C's and D's in their lack of responsibility to their future generations as well as to the contemporary members of their societies.

This fourth point turns on an understanding of the moral significance of inflicting injury on the innocent. The argument would have to go something like this: all else being equal, persons have a right not to be injured or to be made to suffer. To put it another way, causing unjustified suffering to the innocent is immoral. Most of the conceptual issues are hidden in the word "unjustified." The formulation, though, sets the *onus probandi* in terms of respect for the freedom of persons: all else being equal, it is an act of violence against free agents to subject them to suffering or injury (or, for that matter to any state) without their consent. Such imposition would be a circumscription of freedom, and while future persons may be presumed to consent to happiness, they cannot be presumed to consent to pain. (One can always reject happiness while pain, suffering, and injury are usually not so easily foregone.) Moreover increasing the population would injure members of the present population by further decreasing their available resources to the point of ignoring and endangering them, an action which would be immoral for both the societies of C's and D's and any of their members. To subject others to avoidable injury or pain without their consent is to use them as means merely.

The B's would hold that these four propositions are the case even when one society through planning has created a life of great abundance for its members while other societies are close to starving because of failing to control their population.

The C's and D's, though, might argue that such a position would imply that procreating persons could itself be an injury to other persons, that new persons could in their very existence be an injury to already existing persons. This, they might contend, would contradict the notion of obligation to other persons. How, they might ask, could having more free agents be a state of affairs one should prevent, if persons are the cardinal value in morality?

At least three important issues are at stake here:

I. In what circumstances, if any, can one society create obligations for a second society with respect to the first?

II. Are there circumstances in which aiding another society would be wrong because it would lead to the avoidable injury of more persons?

III. What are our obligations to future generations with regard to preventing their suffering (e.g., living in a state of starvation)?

The initial issue is whether one society can impose obligations on another in virtue of the first society's lack of providence. It is one thing to appeal to pity or wish to support the emotion of pity by a general rule which forwards it, and another to say that there is a strict obligation to support an improvident or unlucky society.

Attempts to reconstruct conceptually the meaning of justice, such as offered by John Rawls, generate a notion of a general human community on the basis of which basic obligations exist that include the support of the disadvantaged.[3] Such views construe the world as the possession of the community, and entitlement to particular possessions in terms of a basic sense of justice which would structure (and justify) the distribution of possessions. Alternative views are also possible.[4] For the purpose of this paper I will grant that persons do have a right to receive help from others when such help would not seriously disadvantage the donor and when the person in need of help is not willfully in that state of need.

The limiting conditions on such obligations to help others are what is at stake here. For example, if X could raise a crop and survive easily, but prefers instead to let Y support him and threatens to starve in the absence of Y's support, does it still follow that Y has a duty to support X? Would such be a case of X using Y as a means merely for his own satisfaction? It may indeed follow that under such circumstances Y should not feed X, since in doing so Y would be supporting X in an immoral act of extortion. Though Y may give to X because Y likes X, etc., he should not give because X threatens to starve through indolence unless his support is forthcoming. The argument would be: though one has a duty of beneficence to others, one has a duty not to support violence—the use of persons as means merely —even if that violence is subtle and indirect. To accede to violence (forceful constraint of freedom), at least when other choices are possible, is to endorse violence and thus to endorse actions in opposition to the respect of persons, which in the end must be the source of any strict obligation of beneficence (i.e., of an obligation of beneficence not based simply on the long-run usefulness of beneficence).

A few qualifications are in order. First, clear cases of such extortion for support are probably infrequent; this sketch is meant to present a limiting case as a theoretical possibility (except for one special genre which will be discussed below). Second, the amount of giving by the advantaged to the needy which would significantly disadvantage the donor and thus excuse the donor from giving is left undefined. Third, there may (in qualification of the first caveat) be a special category of cases where persons do improperly create or appear to create obligations for others, namely, by reproducing so as to bring about such a large population that the society itself becomes needy, thus obligating or appearing to obligate other societies to support it—and these are the cases at hand here. As the above suggests, in some of these cases the obligation of beneficence will be defeated or overridden by other obligations. In other cases a society may improperly (by acting negligently) create an obligation for others to aid it (e.g., to supply funds for a tardily implemented but at last sincerely pursued program of birth control).

II. INJURING PRESENT PERSONS WITH MORE PERSONS

How can persons be an injury to persons? The point can be made out in this fashion: (1) one ought not to diminish the common store of food when this would significantly disadvantage others; (2) but increasing the number of persons will significantly disadvantage already existing persons in just this way. Thus, reproduction can under circumstances of restricted resources be a direct injury to already existing persons. In such circumstances one ought not, therefore, increase the number of persons. Present persons can be injured by the production of more persons.

A counter-argument would be that increasing the number of persons cannot be a disvalue since persons are of utmost value; they are the central concern of morality, and thus the more persons in the world, the more value there will be. This argument fails because persons have absolute value only (!) in a very special sense. As moral agents they must be treated as free agents, as ends in themselves to use a Kantian phrase, not because they have an ultimate or absolute exchange or economic value, but because insofar as they exist, they are the ultimate foci of all moral obligations.[5] They can be respected as free agents in addition to being valued or disvalued.

The sense of having an absolute value identifies a person as having moral dignity, being a free agent, but it has no bearing on the market value of persons. It rather gives a grounding for rights and duty language which is not reducible to talk about goods and values; it grounds duties (and thus rights) on the need to respect rational free agents as worthy of praise and blame. In this sense persons are respected, not valued. Therefore it does not follow that increasing the number of persons would increase the amount of value in the world.

Further, a judgment is not precluded concerning what value a future person could add to the community of actual persons.

Rather it specifies that such future persons, should they exist, would have to be treated with respect, that is, not used as means merely. But this would not forbid estimating whether adding another person to the community would have a negative or positive economic value. In fact if states of affairs have value in terms of being valuable for persons, one would seek to achieve that level of population coincident with the best life open to all persons.

Increasing the number of persons or replenishing the present number of persons with new persons, when the existence of such new persons will deprive already existing persons of needed resources, concerns the rights of the already existing persons. Causing there to be new persons under circumstances of extremely limited resources would be an injury to already existing persons. It would deprive them of the requirements for a decent life if not for survival itself. If there is a right to beneficence from others, then there is surely a right to continue to possess those necessities required for one's own decent survival. But increasing population growth will, given limited resources within a particular society, require already existing persons to forego their claims even to some necessities.

To restate this point in terms of the C's and D's, already existing C's and D's have a *prima facie* moral claim against any C's and D's about to reproduce that they not do so in order that the population reestablish itself at a level conducive to a satisfactory lifestyle. For a C or D to reproduce in spite of this claim is, all else being equal, an act of injustice, depriving other C's and D's of a fair claim to a decent lifestyle.

Further, the A's and B's are not obligated to help the C's and D's postpone the consideration of their obligations to the starving members of their own society (i.e., not to procreate more persons to compete for already scarce resources). The A's and B's are not obligated to forego affluence so that the C's and D's can temporarily have sufficient resources to continue population expansion—until everyone is so badly off that any further procreation would not only deny another affluence, but the necessities for life—because the C's and D's have an obligation not to use the A's and B's to postpone their own day of making a reckoning concerning the limits of their population growth. The C's and D's may not oblige the A's and B's to work so that the C's and D's can have more children, unless (as a necessary though not sufficient condition) the A's and B's agree to a changed vision of what would be an optimum lifestyle. Otherwise the C's and D's would be conspiring to use the A's and B's as unconsenting means to their own goals. But there can be no obligation to be used as a means merely—that is, the C's and D's must first recognize their obligation to their own future generations.

To summarize: one society can generate moral obligations for another by expanding its population to the point where its members begin to starve. It can create an obligation on the part of other societies to show beneficence to its starving population. That obligation may, though, be defeated by an obligation not to act to increase the injury done to persons, or by an obligation not to allow one society to use another as a means merely. Nonstarving societies can refuse on moral grounds to contribute to the societies in need: when those starving societies refuse to agree to decrease their population to a level (1) no longer placing them in need, and (2) no longer threatening to maintain or increase the suffering to present persons by increasing the number of persons competing for scarce resources. One society can create obligations for another on the basis of a duty to be beneficent, but that duty does not obtain when the obligating society does not act in good faith to eliminate the burden of that obligation or when that beneficence would increase injury to persons. Thus no society need support a second society when the second society uses the first for its own ends without recognizing its duty either to its own members or to the members of the donating society.

III. INJURING FUTURE PERSONS

The duty not to injure future persons bears special examination. It is a special case of the contention that there is a duty not to contribute to a society if such contributions will lead to an increase in the number of individuals who will be harmed. One is asserting that future persons must be included in calculating the number who will be harmed. If one ought not to cause the amount of human suffering to increase, and if feeding individuals of a starving society will increase the suffering of persons even if these are future persons, then, this argument goes, one ought not so act.

The issue in this part of the argument is difficult because one is talking about future persons being injured by there being too many future persons. Can future persons be distinguished so that one can say which future persons injured which? And what if the excess number are born along with the number of persons who would not be excess—can these groups of future persons be distinguished?

The answer, I will contend, is yes. Until there actually is a person there is no one to be better off or worse off. One can, though, still talk of what one may or may not do which would redound to the injury of such a future person should he or she exist. That is, as soon as one envisages at least one future person, then there is an issue of how many more future persons there can be before a further increase would injure the then existing future persons. The future persons who would be injured are those who would exist should the population have been limited, but who would be injured by its not having been limited. If there are to be any future persons, one owes it to whoever they will be that there not be too many of them.

This argument presupposes that one can decide which possible persons of those who could exist will become actual future persons given certain actions on our part. These possible persons can be specified only in an indeterminate fashion: as the class of those persons that can be born in year X, given resources Y, and a desired lifestyle Z. It presupposes that one can speak of having decided, for example, to have a population of one hundred, so that if one then decided to have a population of one hundred and fifty, one could say that the extra fifty would be an injury to the first one hundred.

To make this distinction one must treat the first one hundred as actual persons who will exist in the future and who would be injured if the next fifty persons were also actual and not just possible future persons. This claim may sound involved, but it is similar to a couple deciding whether to have two children or four children when they only have sufficient funds for two children (and in addition they are using a fertility drug to have them all at once—either as twins or quadruplets). The conception of the two *extra* children would be the beginning of an injury to the first two envisaged children. In short, one can speak of the birth of future persons injuring not only present persons, but also injuring other envisaged future persons.

This argument presupposes that causing another suffering or injury requires justification and that there is no justification for causing future persons to starve or be likewise injured if such injury can be avoided. There is no obligation to cause any particular future person to be; but if one does produce such a future person, one owes that person circumstances that would not be an essential circumscription of the possibilities of human life. Issues lie hidden here that I can only indicate in passing. Though everyone may agree that starvation is a basic circumscription of human life, what of cultural deprivation, etc.? Without wishing to slight such issues I would like to take this much as given: circumstances of starvation and lack of availability of basic shelter and clothing would, in most cases, seriously circumscribe a person's life so that such circumstances should not be imposed on anyone, not even future persons. One should not therefore increase the number of persons so injured, even when that number embraces future persons.

The reader should note that this argument is *not* meant to deny that the affluent have obligations to support the needy, but rather to emphasize that such obligations must be discharged in a responsible fashion, with regard to the effects of the circumstances in which those obligations are discharged. The scope of responsibilities enlarges to include care for future persons. As a result one is obliged to attend to the consequences for future persons of feeding persent persons. Which is to say, one is not simply *excused* from feeding populations which are not engaged in active population control; one rather discovers that *other obligations* can count against engaging in such actions. The obligation not to injure others includes future persons.

IV. The Rights of Future Generations Versus Their Value

In closing something should be said concerning the place of future generations in these considerations. The emphasis here has been on the obligations that exist between affluent and needy societies and between their generations in times of famine, not on issues of values or interests. The intent has been to speak of rights that cannot be reduced to interests in goods or values, such as the right of innocent persons not to be subjected to useless suffering.

But future generations have a value for us as well as having rights. For various reasons we value future generations and the continuation of the species so as to give a direction and purpose

to our lives. We have an interest in there being future generations; but we have no obligation to produce them, for there are
now no future persons whom we at present have an obligation to
cause to come into existence. Such future persons are merely
possible persons. Possible persons do not *now* have a right to be
born, for there is no one to bear that right even if some sense
could be made of such a claim. The actual persons they will be,
when and if they should be, will though have the right to have
been treated fairly should we cause them to come into existence.
What can we make of that right, or for that matter of the
standing of future persons?

If we know that a person will come into existence, we would
want to say that he or she will have a right not to have been
injured by us. An illustration is perhaps helpful: if I fire an
arrow into space such that it will fall to earth years from now
where I know people will be and where it will strike a future
person, that person in that future time will be actual and will
have an actual right not to be injured. Even though the person
who will be injured had no existence when the arrow was fired, it
will be an actual person who will be injured when the arrow
strikes. One will be injuring an actual, not a merely possible,
person. Thus on the one hand, though I have no obligation to
cause there to be future persons, I do have an obligation to try
not to injure those future persons who will in fact be actual
persons. Since my actions can span time and reach beyond my
death to yet unborn persons, my obligations have a similar scope.
To put it a bit more starkly: (1) there is no obligation to have any
future generations, though future generations have a value for
us; (2) if there will be future generations, then we have obligations not to have injured them.

If we will have future generations come into existence, we
then owe those persons who will be members of those generations a life that will not be structured by suffering caused by us,
assuming such suffering can reasonably be avoided by our actions. We are obliged not to do those things which would likely
injure future persons. To put it in terms of limiting population
growth, one would not have a duty to feed a society if the pro-
visions of such food would abet that society in injuring future
persons. Conversely, one would have a duty to invest resources
in population control if such investment were likely to protect

future individuals and would not significantly disadvantage the donor. What will or will not injure future generations is an empirical issue.

The moral is that present actions must be considered not simply in terms of their impact on present persons, but on future persons as well. The injury of not feeding present persons may be outweighed by the very likely injury to even more future persons which would, all else being equal, result from feeding present persons. If one ought to choose to injure fewer persons rather than more persons, then the calculation of the impact of present policies on future persons must be considered. In short, the scope of moral concern must have a future-oriented dimension, a point which Garrett Hardin makes.

This future direction of responsibilities has implications concerning obligations which can only be suggested here: as the obligation to feed the hungry is defeated by circumstances that would lead to greater injury to persons, one incurs an obligation to help to diminish the numbers of the hungry via contraceptive programs, etc., so as to protect future persons. As the first obligation is contravened, the second obligation comes to the fore.

V. CONCLUSIONS

The use of triage language in choosing which societies will or will not be fed is likely to obscure the fact that the moral issue concerns how to do justice to as many persons as possible. The legitimate use of triage language in medicine may include such a goal of justice, though the use of triage language in wartime medicine often has as its focus winning a war, not attending to the just claims of the persons concerned. Moreover, triage language, especially with regard to a lifeboat ethic, can easily be taken to be a triage focused simply on keeping one's own lifeboat comfortable. By focusing on wider obligations, not just interests, I have attempted to substitute a somewhat more complex, and hopefully more accurate, picture of the web of human responsibilities which may oblige us to feed certain societies and not others. This picture should suggest that Garrett Hardin is wrong in holding that we must abandon our present ethical sensitivities in order to survive. On the contrary, one can act to survive by drawing out the implications of the usual ways we talk about our mutual rights and duties, adding only a heightened concern for the effect of our present actions on present and future persons.

NOTES

1. Paul R. Ehrlich and Anne H. Ehrlich, *Population, Resources, Environment* (San Francisco: W. H. Freeman and Company, 1970), p. 301.
2. Garrett Hardin, "Living on a Lifeboat," *Bioscience*, 20 (October 1974), 561–68.
3. John Rawls, *A Theory of Justice* (Cambridge, Massachusetts: Belknap Press of Harvard University Press, 1971).
4. Robert Nozick, *Anarchy, State, and Utopia* (New York: Basic Books, 1974).
5. Immanuel Kant, *Grundlegung zur Metaphysik der Sitten*, in *Kantswerke, Akademie Textausgabe*, vol. 4 (Berlin: Walter de Gruyter and Co. 1968), pp. 434-35.

FAMINE IN THE PERSPECTIVE OF
BIBLICAL JUDGMENTS AND PROMISES

WALTER HARRELSON

FAMINE APPEARS in the biblical literature (Old and New Testaments) both as a natural event with which human beings must attempt to cope and also as a sign of the sin and failure of human beings, especially of the people of God. It must be examined under these two aspects. The points of their inter-section need also to be explored. It seems to me evident that just these two dimensions of world famine also emerge in con-temporary discussions. World famine, on the one hand, is simply a product of the development of life and civilization on our planet, a grievous problem for which some solution must be found if at all possible. On the other hand, the prospect of the destruction of millions of human beings by starvation cannot help but raise the most fundamental of moral questions. Who is to die? How are they to die? How must the life of those who may survive be changed? Is it possible for anyone to survive meaning-fully if a large portion of the human race cannot? In relation to such questions it surely is not amiss to inquire about famine as a result of human sin, and of famine in relation to the hope of the human race for peace and well-being.

FAMINE AS A NATURAL CALAMITY

Almost immediately after Abraham entered into the land of promise and blessing, a famine occurred (Genesis 12:10). The

For eight years Dean of the Divinity School, Mr. Harrelson is currently Distinguished Professor of Old Testament at Vanderbilt University. He chairs the project to microfilm manuscripts of Ethiopian churches and monasteries. His recent scholarly interests are reflected in an article appearing in the forthcoming bi-centennial issue of *Interpretation* under the title, "Knowledge of God in the Church."

patriarch had to seek life in Egypt. The famine is not associated with the sin of God's people; it simply happened. Abraham resorts to such devices and stratagems as occur to him to provide for his family. The same is the case with Joseph (Genesis 37–50). The jealousy of his brothers leads to his being sold into bondage in Egypt. There famine occurs. Joseph's successful interpretation of the Pharaoh's dream of lean years to come leads to his becoming the person to prepare the way for Egypt, and God's people as well, to survive. No special act of revelation is involved; Joseph's wisdom is of course a gift of God, but his exercise of wisdom is what is expected of those who possess the gift. The famine's effects are mitigated and life continues, albeit with new and more severe problems.

These narratives in the Book of Genesis are the product of a way of viewing God's dealings with the peoples of earth and with Israel that became prominent in the tenth century B.C. Similar narrative literature describes the rise of David to the kingship and the struggle over who is to succeed him as king. The literature is marked by an understanding of the workings of God in the world that is distinctive in the religious literature of the ancient world. Human beings are charged to assume responsibility for events in the world, to cope with natural and historical crises, to discern the workings of God in the midst of the movements of nature and history, quiet workings, often mysterious or enigmatic but susceptible of understanding. Human beings have the ability to deal with the problems and issues of life. God is present with them as they do so; his power is at hand. But God does not always interpose that power when it is requested, stepping in to do what human beings will not do. In some senses it is a remarkably "secular" approach to religious understanding, even though the narratives display an authentic belief in the power and presence of God and discern the hand of God in much that transpires.

Famine on this view is one of the great problems human beings face. Pestilence, drought, warfare, disease, earthquakes, and similar events in the life of Israel and of her neighbors offer fundamental challenges to the people, but they are not immediately and directly traced to the displeasure of God or to the sin of individuals or groups. Elijah's theophany at Mt. Horeb (I Kings 19) may be significant in this connection. God is not present in the earthquake, the fire, or the wind that sweep by

Elijah's hiding place. God is present in a "sound of quiet stillness."

The New Testament reflects this same understanding of the calamities that befall human beings. In the parable of the Prodigal Son (Luke 15:11–32) the appearance of famine in the land to which the younger son has wandered is an entirely natural event. Just as God lets the rain fall upon the unjust and the just alike (Matthew 5:45), so also calamities befall persons quite apart from sin or divine punishment for sin. The blind man in the Gospel of John (chapter 9) was born blind not as a consequence of his own or his father's sin. Rather the blindness offered an occasion for the works of God to be disclosed; the question of the cause of the blindness is not pursued at all.

The Israelite wisdom tradition also understands famine and other scourges as natural events. The wise of ancient Israel were convinced that God's good earth was established in an orderly way; nothing in the world order was fundamentally alien to the realization of human ends. It was within the world order, in the human realm in particular, that difficulties arose—fundamentally, difficulties of human understanding. The more optimistic voices of wisdom invited the community to look closely into the structure of things in order to discern what made for good and what for ill. Tragedy there was, perversion of life, human ill; these, however, could be addressed and often surmounted through the application of the power of wisdom. Wisdom was a gift of God, but it was to be claimed and made the more readily accessible through human efforts.Even the more sceptical of the wisdom writers understood the need for human beings to search out the mysteries of God's creation, to come to terms with them, and to find their way in the world. That the author of the poetry in the Book of Job (Job 3:1–41:6) was unable to penetrate the mysterious workings of divine justice was not reason for cursing God and dying; on the contrary the poetry closes with the appearance of God in his mystery and majesty, and with the author's recognition that the struggle for meaning could issue in just such a theophany.

Similarly the author of Ecclesiastes, while discerning that all is vanity and a striving after wind, knows nothing better than to commend the fear of God and fidelity to the will of God. He is able to do so because he knows that vanity too is vanity; the world does have its meaning, life is purposive, its efforts worthwhile to

God. God is simply not pleased to provide the answers to the questions that human beings raise. The struggle for meaning and for blessing must continue, but without false hopes.

FAMINE AS A CONSEQUENCE OF HUMAN SIN

The other view of famine is the more familiar and certainly the more prominent in the biblical literature. The Israelites like their neighbors recognized dark forces at work in the world, afflicting the fields, the herds, and human beings. They also believed in the power of the curse spoken by a person against an enemy, a word of power that carried within itself the ability to damage the one against whom it was directed. The cultic literature of the Old Testament is full of evidences of such an understanding. The theologians of ancient Israel spoke out strongly in support of the unique power of Yahweh and forbade all resort to other powers, including the power of the curse. As a result, the way was prepared for an understanding of calamities as arising almost exclusively from the action of the God of the covenant, sent to punish sinners for their sin. This view in turn had to be challenged since experience taught that sinners often escape the full consequences of their sin, while the relatively righteous suffer far out of proportion to any discernible acts of faithlessness.

FAMINE AS NATURAL EVENT AND AS CONSEQUENCE OF SIN

Israel's prophets bring the two views together. Natural events are indeed natural and have to be faced by persons and groups, their effects mitigated or when possible overcome. Calamities fall upon both the just and the unjust with little discrimination. But famine or pestilence or the sword represent divine warnings that the people of the covenant is, as a people, unfaithful. Amos 4:6–12 is one of the most instructive passages in this regard. The prophet recounts how God sent all kinds of scourges upon his people as summonses to them to repent, to return to God. Amos' catalogue of famine, drought, blight, mildew, pestilence, and warfare may have been understood to refer to natural or historical events of the "neutral" kind mentioned above. Amos does not deny that they are natural events. As natural events, however, they call upon the people to inquire why they have come, what meaning is inherent in them, how they are to be addressed. Certainly Amos would understand that human wisdom is called for to avert them, to mitigate their effects. But he sees something else as required: repentance, a turning to God, an amendment of life, a caring for those in need, public and private righteousness. If they will not repent, then they must prepare to meet God in a new act of judgment.

Other prophets connect human failure to practice righteousness with the decline of earth's productivity. The whole land mourns, according to Hosea (4:1–3), in consequence of Israel's acts of murder, theft, adultery, lying, and swearing. Earth itself is damaged by the sin of those appointed to care for the earth. Sin itself on this view works its consequences into the very fabric of existence, damaging all aspects of life. Famine, blight, pestilence, and the like follow upon the people's faithlessness, not as the result of God's sending them.

FAMINE AND THE BIBLICAL PROMISES

Much of the dynamism of biblical religion derives from its understanding of the future of God's people and of the human race. There are many and varied portrayals of what awaits in the appointed future. In all of them one thing is clear. Famine and related natural and historical crises will arise no more. Some of the most earthy of the pictures simply describe the prodigal bounty of food and the necessities of life (Genesis 49:10–12; Amos 9:13–15). Some speak of a harmony between wild beasts and human beings (Isaiah 11:6–8), others of safety for old persons and children in the streets (Zechariah 8:4–5). Famine is not intended to continue; it must be overcome, and in the appointed future it will be overcome.

Other promises of God connect the fulfillment of God's purpose on earth with the appearance of a new king (Isaiah 9:1–7; 11:1–9; Micah 5:1–5, etc.), with a new Exodus from captivity and a new entrance into the land of the promise (Hosea 2:14–23; Isaiah 40:1–11); with the exaltation of Zion the holy city as the center of blessing in the earth (Isaiah 2:2–4; Micah 4:1–4; Isaiah 40:1–11, etc.); with the giving of a New Covenant (Jeremiah 31:31–34) or a new heart and a new spirit (Ezekiel 36:26–27; 37:1–14) or the pouring out of the Spirit upon all flesh (Joel 2:28–29). In most of these promises the center of fulfillment is God's people Israel, but the passages also indicate that the blessings burst the bounds of the community of the covenant and reach the peoples of earth.

A few of the promises are even more universal in their import. The Servant of the Lord in Isaiah 40–55 is charged to be a light to the nations (42:6). A remarkable passage in Isaiah 19:23–25 speaks of a new highway that will connect Egypt and Assyria and of Israel's being one-third with the other two. God will say on that day, "Blessed be Egypt my people, and Assyria the work of my hands, and Israel my heritage." Zechariah 8:22–23 and 14:16–21 have similar universalistic pictures of the coming day of consummation.

New Testament portrayals of the future are drawn largely from the above Old Testament promises. The heavenly city, the new Jerusalem, is lowered from heaven upon a transformed earth (Revelation 21–22), the Servant of the Lord is the crucified one who bore the sins of many, the long-expected ruler of God's people rules from the cross and from his throne at the right hand of the Father. The time of consummation has broken in upon the world and even now the blessings of the new age are at hand, known in the community of those who name Jesus the Christ as Lord. The public display of righteousness and wholeness of life is near at hand, and persons are eagerly to await its coming as they live in the strength provided in advance of the public display.

While Judaism and Christianity differ fundamentally over the question of the consummation of God's work in the world, both give large place to these promises of biblical religion. The promises indicate the authentic and true character of human life. Life is intended to be marked by wholeness, by peace, by possibilities for all human beings. Food, clothing, shelter, and opportunity for a meaningful existence are purposed by God for all. Famine, therefore, is not God's intention. Where famine exists, the purpose of life remains unfulfilled. Those who believed in the coming time of consummation were under judgment because their own society so poorly resembled the society that God was bringing to birth. They also were given confidence to endure the trials that they faced as they held firmly to faith in the reality of that coming time of blessedness. And they were pulled toward the consummation, drawn and fascinated and lured into as full a realization of the coming day as they were able to embody. Biblical eschatology, therefore, provides one of the driving forces toward the confronting of famine and other ills of earth. Rather than encouraging a passive waiting upon God, it encour-

ages the opposite: active engagement with God in order that the
day of consummation not be so long delayed.

The New Testament stresses the new quality of existence in
the world created in the community of those who know the living
presence of the Lord. This quality of existence is intended,
however, to affect the public life of those who share it. The Old
Testament picture of life in obedience to God's public and private demands in the world is affirmed and intensified in a
faithful Christian community.

FAMINE AND FAITH IN GOD

Biblical religion knows, however, that there are worse things
in the world than famine, dreadsome though it be. Unfaithfulness to God, defiance of his purposes, rejection of Torah,
selfishness, contempt for fellow human beings, pride—all of
these are worse than famine. In Amos 8:11–15, we have a powerful meditation on a coming famine: a famine of hearing the
Word of the Lord. Just as God once sent famine and blight and
pestilence to call the people to repentance, in a day close at hand
God will send a more fearful famine: he will withhold his Word
of guidance, of judgment, of promise. With no word from God,
people will be driven to frenzy. They will run aimlessly throughout the world, desperately seeking that without which they cannot possibly live: God's judging and healing Word.

Thus the Bible knows that sheer human existence does not
suffice: life must be meaningful life. In the New Testament
Jesus is presented as having met the Satan's promise of food for
all with a quotation from the Book of Deuteronomy (8:3): "Man
does not live by bread alone" (Matt. 4:4). Life is more than food
and clothing (Matt. 6:25–33), although God knows that the
community needs food and clothing and shelter. In the final
analysis human life needs purpose, hope, a sense of the mean-
ingfulness of things. Remove these and it is a small thing to be
able merely to survive.

FAMINE IN BIBLICAL PERSPECTIVE: A SUMMARY

Biblical religion therefore depicts famine as a natural calamity
that requres all possible human initiatives for its overcoming.
God created humankind to care for the earth, to release its
powers and goods, and to cherish what God created. God provided understanding, wisdom, discernment to humankind and

expects that these will be exercised in human efforts to be a blessing on the earth. Famine also appears as an instance of the effects of dark and evil powers loose in the world, powers to be averted by all means available. The theological thinkers of ancient Israel combatted such a view, insisting that God's people had to do with God, not with demonic forces. When famine appeared, it was a sign of God's displeasure. Human sin contributed to the emergence of such calamities as famine.

Israel's prophets joined the two views, stressing that God worked through natural events to warn and to guide his people. God required of them public and private righteousness, the care of the poor and the relief of the oppressed. God summoned them to acts of faithfulness, to repentance for misdeeds, to a restoration of communion between them and himself, and between and among one another. He promised that a day lay ahead within which the scourges and evils of life would be swept away, when righteousness and peace would flourish, when the blood-flecked garments and boots of the warriors would become fuel for the fire (Isaiah 9:5). They were to live in the light of such promises, were to exercise all efforts to overcome the tragedies that befell the human community, were to place their final trust in God and in God alone, and were to do his will in the world.

FAMINE IN THE PERSPECTIVE OF BIBLICAL
JUDGMENTS AND PROMISES

We turn now to the question whether this exploration of biblical religion offers any guidelines for the human community currently facing world starvation. Clearly we should not expect a "solution" to the problem of famine. We may find clues, and I believe that we do, for the addressing of several of the most urgent moral questions raised by world starvation.

1. *Famine as a natural event*

It is worthwhile to note that the biblical tradition does not always look for a culprit when famine occurs. In our day it is important first of all to recognize that human beings have to some degree drifted into the current situation. No conglomerate of groups, no particular nations, no individuals have been at work to create famine for the millions. Famine results from the several familiar causes: increased span of life, the growth of population, crop failures, drought, changing weather conditions, and the like. These events are bitterly tragic as they lead to world starvation. They represent a challenge to the human community to overcome them if at all possible. The first thing to do, therefore, is not to assess blame but to marshall all energies and commitments and passions in order to solve the problem, if it can be solved.

2. *Famine as a sign of human failure*

In the second place, however, we are invited by biblical religion to see wherein the human community in fact has gone wrong. Famine is a natural event, but it is also more than a natural event. Biblical religion insists that God charges human beings to care for the earth, to struggle with him in the world for blessing, to see to the needs of the poor and the oppressed and the neglected, to share life and goods with those in need. When we review the history of nations during the last several decades, we certainly see many opportunities missed to raise the standard of life for many millions. Had the standard been raised, the growth of population would not have been so astronomically large, for the felt need of child-bearing in such numbers would have diminished.

Moreover, the blessings of contemporary Western civilization have come at a very high price, a price paid most dearly by those who have been excluded from such blessings. Rampant waste, astronomical military expenditures, exploitation of the goods of earth, gross eating habits, and all the rest of the fundamental evils in the development of industrialized societies have to be identified as contributing to world famine. The gap between the very wealthy and the very poor contributes to world famine, no matter whether its elimination would solve the problem. Thus, the biblical reminder that famine is not unconnected with human sin dare not be ignored.

Given this situation, it is ironic that some proposed steps to ease world famine offer ways of survival not for the victims of oppression and neglect but precisely for those who have failed most signally to check the development of world famine. Despite the generosity of some western nations to poorer nations, the exploiters, the overeaters, the overwealthy, and the ravagers of earth are found largely among those centers of population that probably would survive worldwide starvation, at least for some-time. Withholding food from nations that are overpopulated and continue to bear too many children, and providing food only to those peoples who appear to have a chance to survive and who take action to control births may have a certain logic about it. But it certainly appears odd morally for the persons most responsible for world famine to be the ones to escape its ravages.

Even so, there is not much point in singling out particular peoples for guilt. Biblical religion points to the sin of God's people in particular, because so much responsibility for the care of earth and for the active demonstration of righteousness is believed to lie with them. Famine results as a consequence of the failure of a people, not of particular individuals. And famine hits the community, not just the persons most responsible for its appearance. So also it is today. Famine is a worldwide issue, and it appears as a sign of the failure of the human community to provide for the needs of earth's peoples. Some have borne too many children. Some have ravaged the fields and made them useless. Some have overeaten and overconsumed the goods of earth, wasted precious food and goods of life, lived lavishly and unheedingly. But many of the failures are attendant upon successes. The technological advances have provided manifold increases in the production and distribution of food and other goods. Advances in the health field have prolonged life and removed or mitigated the effects of death-dealing diseases. The creation of new job opportunities, the more humane dealings with people long subject to enslavement or discrimination or poor reward for labor have enabled many to provide more adequately for the needs of their families. These very successes in dealing with problems such as the food supply have helped to create overeating, overconsumption, the draining of the earth's resources, the pollution of its air and streams and soil, and all the rest. For these reasons, famine on the contemporary scene represents a failure of the human community, not merely of some of its parts.

Some are, nevertheless, more responsible than others for the continuing plight of the starving and the ill-fed. Overeating and overconsumption, gross inequality in the control of wealth, and a desire to maintain one's own style of life irrespective of world famine clearly constitute sin in the biblical perspective. The alleviation of the plight of the hungry may well not be possible through a redistribution of the goods of earth, or a check on the consumption of the peoples of certain lands. Even so, redistribu-

tion of earth's goods and reduction of waste are morally inescapable. By any moral standard the present state of affairs is
indefensible and intolerable.

3. *Things worse than death by starvation*

The biblical reminder that there are worse fates than death by
starvation also belongs to our subject. For one thing it is of
fundamental importance to think of persons facing starvation
concretely, not simply as those who inhabit a given part of earth.
They are persons with their own gifts and talents, their own
failings and accomplishments, their own hopes and fears. They
are, in the perspective of biblical religion, human beings created
in the image of God, charged to care for the earth and to be a
blessing. Their lives have purpose, their human accomplishments are real, their values defensible, and their hopes deserving of consideration by others.

Moreover, in any human community one finds just those
qualities of life that make a difference to the human race: active
concern for others, a readiness to suffer for the sake of
righteousness, a commitment to the highest of human ideals and
purposes. No one people deserves to die while other persons
live. If millions are to die, it is important that those who survive
recognize that among the dying are those who affirm qualities of
life that are enduring, that transcend death itself. A sharing with
others as starvation proceeds, support and comfort rendered to
the dying, dying with a sense of the value of life, handing over
life to the author and giver of life—these and other life-affirm-
ing acts that accompany the act of dying enrich the human
community, as they have throughout the centuries and the millennia.

Such a way of dying is not something to be expected or anticipated, of course. It comes mysteriously when it does come.
And there are many, surely, in a starving community who presumably would be driven by the threat of death to seek to
preserve physical life by any means open to them. The point is
that the miracle does in fact occur, and some know in the act of
dying how to die a good death, and do so.

And on the other side, living a bloated, gorged life while
others starve; amassing wealth beyond any human need; grasp-
ing after power and position and privilege for no human end

—living such a life and dying represent something loathsome to the human community. Such a death is qualitatively worse than death by starvation of the relatively innocent.

Dying to no purpose, dying with no sense of the meaning of life, dying heedless of others or self-pityingly—such a death may well be worse than death by starvation. Dying purposively, giving up life for others, facing death resolutely and confidently, dying "in the Lord" are ways of dying that biblical religion understands and commends. Should such a death come by starvation, it would be a death that illuminates and affirms life.

The point of these observations is not by any means to mitigate the tragedy of the anticipated death of millions by starvation. It is only to underscore the fact that, as the millions die, there will be those among them who know what life is all about and who will have a witness of importance to the living (if they can hear it) as well as to those among whom they die. And it is to remind those who may well be among the survivors that survival at the expense of others may be more tragic than to die with them.

4. *Starvation and Repentance*

The biblical admonition to those under the threat of starvation, of military invasion, of loss of life by any means is a direct and simple one: "Repent!" It is a real question whether this central element in biblical religion can be effectively spoken of on the contemporary scene. Repentance for biblical religion involved more than an attitude, more than an act of the will. It meant a turning from the path that was destructive of life to the path that issued in life's enhancement. It meant an end to the exploitation of persons and action that aimed at their welfare. It meant sharing goods with those in need, actively pursuing righteousness. It meant responsible sharing of the work of earth, seeing to earth's needs, contributing to the realization of God's purposes for his people and for all peoples.

In biblical times persons and groups often were driven to repentance by adversity. Not always and not even very often was there some spontaneous conversion, some turning to God in glad delight at the newly discovered love and forgiveness of God. Repentance came about under the pressure of the life of the people of God. Suffering in consequence of sin, suffering with God in adversity, struggling with God for blessing and renewal of life—such settings more often than not produced the turning to God's intended way.

It may be so today. World famine presents such a challenge to the entire human community. Those nearest to death by starvation are not far removed from the remainder of the human community today. The millions will not die unnoticed. No wall can hide their dying from the surviving, just as no wall can finally protect the more fortunate from the starving. World community, a common international commitment to share the goods and possibilities of life on the planet, may well be forced upon the human community in consequence of world famine. Such a world community would not arise without inequity, without constraints upon human freedom, without serious dislocations within the various social structures of contemporary nation states. But its emergence might be the only way in which life can be maintained on the planet.

Repentance in the face of world starvation is not in my judgment a pointless proposal. Doing acts that indicate one's complicity in the actions that have produced world famine is a possibility of groups and nations as well as of individuals. Words of repentance are important, but deeds demonstrating repentance are more important and more credible. The rich nations of earth can cut down their consumption, reduce prodigal waste, live more sanely and soberly. The starving will not immediately reap the benefits of such action, of course, but as a sign of active repentance for the existence of world famine such steps would be of enormous symbolic and eventually of actual practical value. One thing is certain: if dozens of millions of human beings are to die by starvation in the next several years or decades, then none can survive such a loss of human life who have not done acts of repentance: reducing waste, caring for the poor and the oppressed, sharing their goods, adopting a style of living more nearly commensurate with the tragic fate befalling the human race. Apart from such repentance, the only differance between the living and dead would be that some would die sooner than others; life on the planet would have become unendurable and therefore impossible.

5. *Starvation and the promise of God*

The biblical passages portraying the coming consummation of life on earth also have their word to say about starvation. They underscore, as we have noted already, that God purposes a rich and full life for all the inhabitants of earth—his own people and all the peoples of earth. In such a time as ours, it may not be readily possible to reaffirm before the peoples of earth that this biblical vision is sure to come to our planet. It is possible, however, for all to see in the vision the direction in which human life must move. Nothing short of a world community marked by righteousness and equity, by peace and the fullness of human life can, I believe, be the goal of human striving and hoping and dreaming. The scourges of famine, warfare, disease, meaninglessness in life must be overcome. Biblical religion insists that the history of the human race moves forward toward such a goal. What prevents its realization is twofold: human beings will not exercise the ingenuity and wisdom at their disposal to bring in the day of consummation under the impulse from the creator and redeemer; and human beings entrap themselves in sin through acts of injustice and unfaithfulness, and will not turn to God and be set upon the true path once more. Both failings block the realization: a faulty exercise of wisdom and ingenuity, and a perverse misuse of the gifts of life.

These deterrents will not finally succeed, however, according to biblical religion. The New Testament boldly insists that in the new community of faith already they are being radically overcome. Judaism is more modest: fidelity to God's teaching, to Torah, will usher in the kingdom of blessedness and peace, and the community of faith must therefore practice Torah more diligently, more faithfully, more hopefully and confidently than ever before.

Whether or not contemporary peoples can find the way to affirm such confidence in the certainty of the consummation that awaits, all peoples can see in this biblical vision that which *must* come to pass. A renewed commitment to struggle to the death for the realization of such a vision is certainly in order. Life must move in that direction, not in any other. On the path toward the consummation of the purpose of life on earth lies the possibility of a renewal of commitment of peoples and individuals to one another that will enrich life, give it character and tone, make worthwhile the struggles, the suffering, the privation, the new forms of life together that clearly await us all.

Biblical religion also makes clear that there is One present with individuals and groups as they engage in this struggle for peace and wholeness and blessing. The creator and redeemer of life does not merely look on as the struggle proceeds; God is present with the people, enduring their privation, sharing their pain, suffering with them, warning, guiding, encouraging, and forever reaffirming that the promise will come to birth. I believe that this element also belongs in the center of our discussion of world famine. What makes life worth living; what makes dying for the sake of fellow human beings meaningful; what sustains us in the struggle that the blessing may yet come is this interior awareness of fundamental meaning and goodness and blessing even now present in human life. The psalmists of Israel, Israel's prophets and wisemen, the church's apostles and saints all knew this reality. "Whom have I in heaven besides thee? And what is there on earth that I desire other than thee? My heart and my flesh may fail, but God is the strength of my heart and my portion forever!" (Psalm 73:25–26). And the apostle knows that there is nothing in all creation that can separate him from the reality of the love of God (Romans 8:38–39).

Conclusion

Viewed in the perspective of biblical judgments and promises, world famine appears as a natural event requiring human initiatives, ingenuity, wisdom, and perseverance for its alleviation. It is seen also as a consequence of the failure of human beings to claim their proper humanity and live in communion with God and with fellow human beings. Persistence in sin or refusal to exercise the God-given human faculties not only will permit famine and such other scourges to continue; it will cause their acceleration. Nothing short of a world community marked by righteousness and peace and possibility of life for all peoples will suffice. World famine thus represents a delay of the consummation, a delay that must be averted. Famine and other calamities may wreak their damage, but justice and wholeness for the entire human community await, beckon, and will come. In the meantime the peoples of earth are to turn to the source and ground of all meaning and all blessing; are to amend their ways; are to struggle to overcome famine; and are to live in the power of one who is never absent from the living or the dying and always summoning his people to life in community, life for all.

Biblical religion thus invites human beings to seek to preserve all life; to find a solution to world hunger; to recognize that repentance opens the way to life; to bear in mind that some cannot live at the expense of others; that we live together or perish together; and that living or dying we are the Lord's.*

*I wish to thank my colleagues, Professor Lou H. Silberman and James L. Crenshaw, for reading the manuscript and for making many helpful suggestions. I must assume responsibility for the use made of their valuable insights.

FAMINE AND INTERDEPENDENCE:
Toward a New Identity for America and the West

JAMES SELLERS

P ROPONENTS OF "LIFEBOAT ETHICS" argue that, since there likely will not be enough food to match population growth, rich countries should help only those poor countries that seem able to reciprocate by cutting back their birth rates. The others should be abandoned—refused admittance to the metaphorical "lifeboat"—lest the food be spread too thin and the survival of all be imperiled.

Garrett Hardin, one of the more effective spokesmen for the lifeboat metaphor, claims that *"Every life saved this year in a poor country diminishes the quality of life for subsequent generations."* He questions both giving more food indiscriminately and letting those from poor nations immigrate to affluent countries, for "unrestricted immigration moves people to the food, thus speeding up the destruction of the environment in rich countries." It is easy enough to see why poor people should want to move, "but why should rich hosts encourage it?"[1]

Furthermore, one infers, there should be no doubt concerning to whom the food belongs. It belongs to the rich countries. Hardin cites the dictum of William Foster Lloyd, a nineteenth-century British architect of lifeboat ethics:

> "To a plank in the sea, which cannot support all, all have not an equal right; the lucky individuals, who can first obtain possession, being

Mr. Sellers is David Rice Professor of Ethics at Rice University, Houston, Texas. He has given special attention to the role American culture and history play in shaping our moral outlook. His most recent books include *Public Ethics: American Morals and Manners* (1970) and *Warming Fires: The Quest for Community in America* (Seabury, 1975).

justified in appropriating it to themselves, to the exclusion of the remainder."[2]

Lifeboat ethics thus advances three claims. There will not be enough food to match population growth. The source of the problem is the poor countries. Rich nations have ownership rights to the food.

I accept none of these claims, though I agree substantially with the premises of the arguments. I contend, however, that the direst of our dilemmas is not so much food scarcity, or even the frightening spectre of population growth. Rather, our chief difficulty lies at an even deeper level. These current difficulties ultimately question the "fundamental myth" of a people, of a civilization—in this case Western civilization and especially America. Our present quandary calls into question what we make of ourselves as human beings, what it takes to give us a satisfying identity and direction, and how we treat one another morally, politically, and socially.

Thus, far more crucial in dealing with the prospect of world famine than a crash model of distributive ethics is a re-examination of the myths and metaphors which govern the lives of those of us in America and the West—myths which we have taken as the source of our ethics and moralities. Far more useful for getting through the crisis than a wildly mismatched model of triage drawn from medicine, is a phenomenology of interdependence drawn from our evolutionary experience—namely, that man emerged from the prehominoids when he learned to share both the labor of his hunt and the meat that came from it. Far more to the point than the self-serving image of ourselves as a nutritional "lifeboat," able to decide whom and whom not to take aboard, is a long overdue recognition of the wastefulness of the West, led by America. Far from being the world's lifeboat, America and the West, lacking any new self-understanding, will turn out to be the world's *Titanic*, dragging down with us the remainder of our global society.

What we require, in short, is a renewed search for symbols and myths that will let us *be*, and be ourselves, without having to put out contracts on others. The precise nature of that requirement will emerge as we examine the strengths and weaknesses, not only of "lifeboat ethics," but of two leading alternative approaches to the food crisis as well.

I. Nattering Nabobs of Nutrition:
Chiliasts, Technocrats, and Moralists

After experiencing a religious conversion, William Miller, a nineteenth-century Vermont frontiersman, spent two years pondering the Scriptures. "I was thus brought," he announced later, "to the solemn conclusion that in about twenty-five years . . . all the affairs of our present state would be wound up."[3]

Miller thought the end should come in 1843 or 1844. As late as 1914 his successors were still gathering in expectation of the end of the world—only to see the world disappointingly go on with its wars, uncertainties, miseries, and hopes.

It is not difficult to find analogous prophecies among the disquisitions of those who succeed Thomas Malthus today.

The first report of the Club of Rome, *The Limits to Growth*, for example, draws a picture of catastrophe ahead within a hundred years and speaks of forthcoming "modes of collapse"—disappearance of resources, aggravated pollution, and famine. There is a proviso, to be sure: all this is coming unless we perform miraculous about-faces in politics and ethics.

"The race between population growth and food production has already been lost," says Paul R. Ehrlich, a biologist. By 1985 hundreds of millions will starve—"unless plague, thermonuclear war, or some other agent kills them first."

"We are only a few moments from the end of the orgy . . ." is Garrett Hardin's succinct way of putting it.[4]

Let us fully comprehend what is being discussed here: this is word of the approaching end. It is not talk of economic cycles, of ying and yang, of the ups and downs of history. It is a message like William Miller's. It is talk of *finis*. Wilfred Beckerman of the University of London has come up with a phrase for such prophets. He calls them "eco-doomsters."[5]

If indeed this is what they are talking about—end, *finis*—then they are addressing something unique, something unexampled, something unparalleled in human experience. Precisely for this reason the borrowed notion of "triage" is inappropriate. The medical triage officer presides over an emergency in which there is a scarcity of resources—doctors, drugs, or time. So far, so good. But this officer acts on the basis of accumulated experience, on the basis of scores or hundreds or thousands of such cases in the past, in which he or his colleagues more often have been right than wrong.

To apply the triage model to the food crisis is thus an absurdity. Eco-doomsters are talking about something that has never happened before: catastrophic worldwide resource depletion, pollution, famine: viz., the end of the world. Where is the cumulative experience that would enable us to sort out, at such a *dénouement*, whole nations? Who would be qualified for this millenial triage duty? There are fragmentary past cases, of course, such as the Irish potato famine—but these are so far parts of the ups and downs of history, not examples of terminal global collapse.

Quite apart from the singular inadequacy of triage as a model for "the end of all that is," however, is an even graver complaint against the doomsters. It is not that they are wrong in warning us of approaching danger, or even in predicting the end. The problem is that they misapprehend what the end is like. They are talking chiliasm, in short, when they should be talking eschatology.

Chiliasts show up in Christian annals as doom-announcers who are overly eager to quantify the notions of damnation and salvation—that is, they love to put numbers on theological concepts (chiliasm is a derivative of *chilioi*, the Greek term for "thousand"). Chiliasts were hung up on the millenium: at its end, Christ would come, sort out the saved, put an end to history, and reign henceforth with his saints in glory. Or, in another version, this new age, instead of following a thousand-year countdown, would usher in the millenium (again, of the sorted-out saints). In either case the result was to quantify a conception that more profound theologians from St. Augustine to Rudolf Bultmann understood to deal more with the quality of *finis* than with its predictability in time.

Lifeboat ethics is clearly a form of ecological chiliasm. There is the same tendency to take a dire truth that we should heed—that the earth and its resources are finite—and reduce this message of finitude to a quantitative prediction. There is another curious parallel. Both types of chiliasts see the world divided at the end into saved and lost. For the Christo-chiliasts the saved were those who chose Christ early. For the eco-chiliasts the saved are those who do the good works of population control and agronomic stewardship.

There is doubtless an eschatological truth hidden here: Judgment is coming. But it is one that hangs over all of us, not just (as in Lloyd's example) those swimming for the nearest spar. Indeed, most of the decisions to lead a new life are going to have to be made not by the swimmers, but by those in the so-called lifeboat.

The fallacy of chiliasm is that the prophet of finiteness is finite himself, limited in his ability to set a time for the end and even more so in his ability to draw a line between the saved and the damned. I defer to later points in this paper my reasons why Hardin's "drawing of the line" must be rejected. In the meantime we can properly accept a challenge from his message. This challenge is for us to see the judgment and crisis not so much in quantitative as in existential terms. Reworked, the message is (or ought to be) this: in a crowded and finite world, the question of how we shall treat each other assumes new and dramatic importance. As self-evaluation must always precede universal judgment, however, we are therefore summoned to re-examine our deepest convictions about our identity.

Two other approaches to the world food crisis also may be examined. The first is that of the "technocrats." These analysts tend to argue, against the doomsters, that for the time being or even longer there is enough food, or enough arable land to produce enough food. "Contrary to popular preconceptions," writes Goeffrey Barraclough, "there is ample land available to provide food for a burgeoning world population." Citing the calculations of demographer Roger Revelle, Barraclough avers that the world could feed ten times or more its present population. Similarly, Emma Rothschild says that the food problem "is political and economic, and it could have been avoided."[6]

All sorts of technological gains are being reported. New varieties of corn, wheat, and rice give greatly improved yields. Some countries (such as the Peoples' Republic of China) that have been chronically affected by population overgrowth and famine have learned to control their birth rates and to feed the people. With good weather, such agricultural giants as the United States can still produce record grain crops (as in 1975), thus having "wheat running out of our ears."[7]

The technocrats also challenge the Malthusian doctrine that feeding the poor nations only increases the misery of overpopulation and hunger. If people in overpopulated areas were assured of food, this argument goes, this assurance would negate the insecurity which drives people to bring about the birth of extra sons as survival insurance. Alan Berg cites encouraging trends even in such lands of teeming millions as India. In the South Indian state of Kerala, the birth rate dropped over a ten-year period from 37 per 1,000 to 27 per 1,000. Berg's main argument is a moral one, but enroute to his conclusions he makes the technocratic case that it is well within the power of all working together "to produce enough food to prevent masses from starving."[8]

What are the liabilities of the technocratic approach to the food crisis? One, obviously, is that Malthus may yet turn out to be right and the technocrats wrong. I remain uneasy and unconvinced by technocratic calculations that there is enough arable land to feed, say, thirty or forty billion people. I am with the technocrats up to a point, but not up to that point.

Malthus himself expressed these forebodings: "The perpetual tendency in the race of man to increase beyond the means of subsistence is one of the general laws of animated nature which we can have no reason to expect will change."[9] Today, after two centuries in which Malthus' view seemed refuted—two centuries of technological progress—there is need for a new perspective. We need not join the chiliasts in projecting doom. What we must appreciate are the dangers of a purely technological answer to the crisis.

Food may be necessary, and the technocratic operation well may be able to get it for us. But if the chiliasts tend to underestimate the limits of human productivity, the technocrats tend to overestimate them. Our finitude intrudes in both cases, and of the two, perhaps that of the technocrats is the more dangerous. It is all too easy to fall back on *hubris*, mistaken self-elevation.

The technocrats miss the essence of salvation. Food is a means to it. But something more must be grasped if we are to see what human beings really must possess to become fully human. They need the gifts of reunion, mutuality, and resonance. Food and the human spirit presuppose one another. Human concern is also a means to more food. If we are to have enough food we must, paradoxically, seek first that which depends on more food: human interaction. We can lift our sights to provide enough food not just by setting out more tractors, but by tearing down the barriers that leave food stockpiled in one locale and scarce in another.

To the extent that the technocratic approach is identified with the now-battered doctrine of unlimited progress or with the call for perpetual growth, it underwrites a losing myth. There is, however, a message in the technocratic dictum that man can, by his initiative and dexterity, face his crises and hope to overcome them.

In criticizing the technocrats we have edged toward a third approach to the food crisis, that of the moralists. This last group argues that, while chiliastic pessimism is not in order, technocratic acumen alone is not enough. What we really face is a call of conscience. If there is enough know-how to produce the food, and if doing so would solve the problem, then we are morally obligated to act. "After all the political and economic arguments," says Alan Berg in a summary of this position, "dealing with hunger and malnutrition is a moral issue—that demands a moral response."[10]

To follow a moral imperative, Berg argues, need not be understood as a renunciation of self-interest. For most of us, a sense of well-being demands that we act out ethical values in some form of service. We might even go so far as to say that carrying forward such values is "a legitimate rationale for government action."

"Given the facts," Berg concludes, "adherence to the lifeboat or triage theories is an intellectual and moral cop-out." We have no choice but to try to see that the food goes around. "To do otherwise would reflect a fundamental and grievous change in the character of man."[11]

The moralist approach, while it directly counters chiliasm, does not reflect a similar kind of opposition to the technocratic approach. The moralist, in fact, is betting on the technocrats. He is saying, in effect, that the technocrats have better crop reporters and demographers than do the chiliasts, and he is also gambling that the technocratic obsession with growth can be curbed. Indeed, it is precisely in running these risks that his approach becomes a moral one. Given a dispute on the facts —either we can or cannot raise enough food, and either it will or will not help reduce birth rates—he chooses those assumptions that support brotherhood. He is aware of the risk he runs.

The moralist, however, is no pawn of the technocrats. He is the technocrats' critic, pointing out what is missing. The goal of technology is not a mindless extension of progress, nor is it charity, welfarism, and "hand-outs." The goal is to enable us to commit ourselves to one another, for that is the only way we are enabled to live decently.

It is quite possible, of course, to endorse both the technocratic solution and the moralist's rationale at once. Henry Kissinger, for example, told the World Food Council that the realities of the food crisis "summon man to a new test of his capacity and his morality."[12] If one is truly committed to doing something, this would appear to be a good combination.

But there are pitfalls in the moralist's approach. One of them is prematurely to raise hopes with moral assurances before action can be guaranteed. For an American Secretary of State to cite William Faulkner and Thomas Mann and to speak of moral imperatives does not, it must be admitted, actually put food in anyone's mouth. In fact, the interval between a moral call for action and its implementation is often distressingly long.

> The Secretary's speech, with its emphasis upon moral issues, was disappointing to many of the thousands of people who crowded into the Plenary Hall to hear him, for he did not name an amount of money or of grain, by which the United States would increase its food aid.[13]

Another pitfall, even more dangerous, is the illusion of the idealist that moral pleading *alone* could solve our problems —that a few more sermons on love would bring in the day of racial brotherhood, for example. Reinhold Niebuhr condemned a sentimental moralism that "seemed to believe that the only reason men had not followed the love commandment in the vast collective relations of mankind was because no one had called their attention to the necessity."[14]

Garrett Hardin also points to such weaknesses as these. Moral suasion and calls to conscience, he says, are ineffective. If we used signs at intersections that said "PLEASE STOP," meaning "no force will be used, no punishments handed out; we're appealing to your conscience," we know what would happen. The man without a conscience won't stop. Coercion, then, is the only alternative. "A 'PLEASE STOP' sign will not work: we must say 'STOP'."[15]

Hardin's approach, however, is as one-sided as the sentimental moralist's. Though he certainly knows better, Hardin tries to limit us to an either-or choice for attacking environmental problems: moral suasion (which won't work) or force (which will). What Reinhold Niebuhr once wrote of political action applies equally to solving the food crisis. Effective strategy in either case involves what Niebuhr calls "a combination of coercive and persuasive factors. Sentimental moralism which underestimates the necessity of coercion, and cynical realism which is oblivious to the possibilities of moral suasion are equally dangerous to the welfare of mankind."[16]

Perhaps we cannot change the fact that human groups, including nations, are selfish and will, first of all, want to protect their own interest. But there is a difference between "natural" selfishness and "diabolical" selfishness, a difference between "wise" self-interest and "stupid" self-interest.[17] Here is where the real strength of the moralist's approach is to be found. Realistic ethical values can help us to find that elusive difference, and to stay within the limits of a healthy self-interest. In the case of the food crisis, the moral appeal that is needed would remind us that to feed ourselves may be only natural, but to refuse to share with starving nations may be both diabolical and stupid.

Thus far I have argued that ethical values, despite pitfalls, might guide us in the food crisis. We now come to the greatest difficulty of all. Simply stated, it is this: whose morality should be appealed to? After all, the doomsters speak of ethics, too. The spokesmen of the Club of Rome "favor moral change, and the generation of a new 'supreme ethics of survival'."[18] The title of Hardin's book, *Exploring New Ethics for Survival,* shows that, when he demeans such moral entities as conscience and good will, he is simply setting aside somebody else's values in favor of his own.

That is the main reason we cannot be satisfied with a moral approach to the food crisis. We should be left arguing until the end over whose morality is to be accepted, mine or yours.

II. The Way Back Into the Ground of Our Lives:
Of Survival, Responsibility, and Metaphors

What are the deepest-running beliefs, symbols, and myths that have set the identity of the West, especially America? If we obtain some clues at this foundational level, we shall be able to move ahead and rethink a morality that is built up from these roots. This search will be facilitated by considering three fundamental questions:

1. Is *survival*, as the chiliasts claim, really our deepest value, or is there another way in the Western and American tradition of thinking of the meaning of life?

2. Could it be that some of the values we have assumed as the roots of our civilization are themselves partly *responsible* for the food crisis?

3. Which *metaphor* is best for capturing the spirit of our human enterprise in America and the West? The chiliasts say it is that of the lifeboat. Is there a better one, both for dealing with the food crisis and for shaping our identities?

1. Survival

"As a scientist," says Garrett Hardin in the preface to *Exploring New Ethics for Survival*, "I wanted to find a scientific solution." But the population problem turns out to be something of a different order. It is in part a matter of committing oneself to certain values and of rejecting others—all this before technical strategies come into play. Hardin decided that the problem required his "repudiating certain ethical beliefs," as well as "some of the political and economic arrangements" of our society.[19]

Let me be as clear as is Hardin. The ecological standards he wants are healthy for all of us. He wants pollution of air and sea stopped, by whatever forceful means necessary. So do I. He wants population controls, with teeth in them. So do I. He wants the American and Western religion of progress and endless growth condemned as lethal. So do I. We differ principally over our respective choices of the older "ethical beliefs" that now, according to Hardin, must be discarded.

We have already had occasion to notice one of these. Reliance on conscience fails because "a system that depends only on conscience rewards the conscienceless."[20] We must at the same stroke (says Hardin) give up that most longlived of American principles, celebrated by Tocqueville and others, voluntary-ism—the idea that some good and much of the world's work may be accomplished by persons assumed to be capable of voluntary response.

Given our current predicament, still another ethical principle of long standing must be dropped, that which moral philosophers call "distributive justice" (in simple language, the teaching that available goods should be handed out fairly). It is a notion that goes back at least to Aristotle and it has had a distinctive American form. The average American, fortunate in both achievement and resources, has never been exactly willing to give all his goods to the poor and become a friar. But he has, in his national persona, more or less sought to strike a balance between his own good fortune and the needs of the less fortunate. American food relief saved millions of lives after World War I, perhaps five million in Russia alone. The Marshall Plan, admittedly a project with dimensions of American self-interest, helped Western Europe back to prosperity after World War II.

Now, however, we are told that we need another philosophy. If "in nature the criterion is survival," then one thing is certain: "Injustice is preferable to total ruin."[21]

What is left of American and Western morality after such ideals as conscience, the balance between voluntaryism and coercion, and distributive justice have been sacked—all in the name of survival? Nothing, other than survival itself. What we must ask is whether survival—naked survival—is a sufficient moral end, or whether meaningful human existence must not demand more than that.

I do not wish to question the cruciality of survival. I do not doubt, as Hardin says, that "No generation has viewed the problem of the survival of the human species as seriously as we have."[22] I do not argue for a moment that the New Testament ethic of laying down one's life for another can characterize the foreign policy of nations.

What I must question is the tacit isolation of survival as the only (or highest) ethical value. Survival can be a crucial concern without having to be the moral *summum bonum*. Survival can be basic and still not be an obsession that takes away our humane side. If survival is enthroned morally, then human life itself is demeaned. It moves from something natural to something diabolical.

We should beware of any ethic that isolates and enthrones one value. Theologians who raise *agape*, or love of neighbor, to this pinnacle risk losing the weapon of justice and the possibility of enforcing laws and sanctions against the unjust. In a symmetrically opposite way, those who exalt survival risk losing the vision that the goal of life is not merely guaranteed further existence (though it might include something like that). The goal of life is rather community, mutuality, and reconciliation.

If we want to speak of a *summum bonum* that goes to the root of the idea of humanity in America and the West, I contend it would embrace a sense of pluralism, in which we respect each other's identities and cooperate and share in order to enhance those identities. Measured by such a *summum bonum*, a nation that insures its continuance by cutting off others or willing their destruction as a means to the end of survival is no better, ethically, than a tribe of cannibals.

Are we really ready to will the deaths by famine of those in poor nations, as the logic of lifeboat ethics suggests? That some people, maybe millions, could die of starvation in the next generation or so is not the issue. That tragedy *may* occur whether we help or not. The issue is whether we would be willing to *let* it happen, to withhold our help, all in the pursuit of our own survival.

Who is to say that American lives are worth more than African or Bangladesh lives? Even without the promptings of lifeboat ethics, accepting the death of those far away is easy. "Three Million May Die in Africa Drought." That headline appears on page four of section four of my afternoon paper—buried. Surely we do not need any "new ethics" that urges us in the direction that self-interest already propels us. What we need, rather, is an ethics that warns us of the ultimate shipwreck of meaning and identity that comes with a survival-at-all-costs attitude.

"A world that would choose Garrett Hardin's options is a world in which I for one would not care to survive," says Richard Neuhaus, a New York Lutheran clergyman.[23]

I wonder if Hardin himself finally accepts the cold principle of survival. Toward the end of his book, he tells us that population control must be sought in order to preserve "human dignity."[24] On that point, as on many others, I agree with him. But "human dignity" should also be one of the principles by which Americans and others in rich nations are governed, and this surely means that we cannot be satisfied with an ethics of survival. We must seek something more ample, that indeed would look to protect our own interests, but that would also recognize the human enterprise as an irrevocably cooperative one. This, I contend, is the minimum necessary for assurance of human dignity.

2. *Responsibility*

A second basic question is that of responsibility for the predicament. The neo-Malthusians, as we have seen, focus upon the overpopulated poor countries. Food sent to them will just make the problem worse. Since it is our food, we can attack the problem by withholding it. I regard this view of the problem as wrong because it places responsibility in the wrong place. It also makes disastrous assumptions about who may do what with the food.

I begin with the claim that the food belongs to the rich countries. It is certainly tautologically true that American wheat raised in the American Midwest is American wheat—and that American farmers may sell it to whomever they please. But if we recast the issue in the framework of economic and political realism, the claim of ownership turns into a very shaky half-truth.

Suppose we do say apodictically that the wheat is ours and that we are going to withhold it from nations of starving people. What is to prevent, at that juncture, Saudi Arabia and its OPEC partners from cutting off oil shipments to Europe, holding the European industrial machine hostage until we yield up the wheat? After all, if it's our wheat, then it's their oil. What is to prevent countries that control most of our present sources of various vital minerals from simply turning off the flow? The United States, of late, has been almost entirely dependent on imports for its supplies of manganese, cobalt, chromium, titanium, miobium, strontium, and sheet mica. It is only somewhat less dependent than that on imported aluminum, platinum, tin, tantalum, bismuth, fluorine, asbestos, and mercury.[25] Much of this material comes from poor and underdeveloped countries. If they followed the advice that the lifeboat ethicists offer the rich nations, global chaos would soon result.

This is but a crude example, drawn from the industrial realm, of the deeper truth that interdependence, always a mark of the human condition, now has become a *sine qua non* of meaningful existence. The grain may indeed be ours—to sell, store, or feed to animals. But is also *not* ours—to withhold when others are starving. At one time, not so long ago in American history, it effectively might have been ours in every sense. There was a day when the United States could ordain its course and dispose of its resources simply because it was powerful enough to get away with almost anything. But that day is gone. Ecologists like Hardin who keep talking about the organic nature of the environment should readily understand the organic nature of the human enterprise. For better or worse, we are firmly interlocked with all of the others.

Once the illusions of food ownership are disposed of, we may turn to the question of active responsibility for the food crisis itself.

Why are the poor nations so poor? They are, after all, well endowed for the most part with raw materials. They have huge pools of labor. Developed, they would make tempting consumer markets. Let us not rule out a strong measure of self-responsibility. On the other hand, there is ample evidence that the poor nations are kept that way to a degree by activities in America and the West, especially through the operations in these countries of international corporations.

Such corporations might well, we could imagine, function as positive forces in countries to which they come to mine, to farm, or to manufacture. They might well, we could imagine, aid their host nations in becoming developed. That such is not the case is demonstrated by Richard Barnett and Ronald Müller in an analysis of the problem for the *New Yorker*. An essential ingredient for development that is still missing, even where the international corporations have located, is knowledge and expertise.

> A country can have rivers of gold and thousands of potential workers ready to mine it and yet be on the brink of starvation if it lacks the know-how to exploit its natural riches.[26]

The global corporations have taught the citizens some things, to be sure—such as how to operate machinery. But too often the corporations and the advanced nations they represent have not gone on to help the poor countries develop higher echelons of know-how, the kinds of knowledge that would lead to the establishment of schools, local enterprise, and improved social organization. Poor countries are not encouraged to develop structures to generate more wealth that could be kept and recirculated in the local economy. They are not shown how to process their own resources indigenously.

Instead, profits from the branch operations in the poor countries are "siphoned off to the developed world, first as plunder and then in the more respectable form of dividends, royalties, and technical fees." They have been used "to finance the amenities of London and Paris and the industrial expansion of affluent societies."[27] These critics illustrate that, in the mid-1960's, American companies in Latin America took over half their profits back to America—even though more than half the investment funds the companies used in the first place were borrowed locally.[28]

Multinational corporations, operating in effect as agents of America and other developed western nations, have exacerbated the hunger problem in more subtle ways as well. They control more and more arable land in the poor countries. What use is made of it? In Colombia, American landholders may elect to grow carnations, which bring a million pesos per hectare per year, instead of wheat or corn, which bring only a fraction of that sum. The European nations import about a third of the African peanut crop for livestock feeds.[29]

The companies also begin to influence the diet habits of their host peoples through advertising, often in destructive ways:

> Bread becomes a substitute for *tortillas*. . . . There may be some gain in protein and vitamins, but there is a loss in calcium. . . . Coca-Cola, nutritionally speaking, is a way of consuming imported sugar at a high price.[30]

Indeed, it is America and the West which, in many ways, should be the major locus of the world food crisis. Frances Moore Lappé contends that it is we, "the rich world," who most have strained earth's farming capacity. The advanced countries have only about a third of the world's people, but they consume two-thirds of the food. As an example she cites the amount of grain fed American livestock. It is as much "as all the people in China and India eat in a year." This enormous waste is part of "The Great American Steak Religion."[31]

The average steer will use up in feed about twenty-one pounds of feed grain to produce a pound of protein in beefsteak. Do Americans need all of the protein they ingest? No, says Lappé: The average American eats about twice as much as his body needs or can use. The whole system is a monumental waste machine. It is ritualized, systematic waste—"so ingrained in our agricultural practices and in our attitudes and nutritional doctrine that we are all but blind to it."[32]

At this point we encounter one of the primal values of the

American tradition that, however harmless or even useful it once might have been, is now clearly central to the crisis. It is the American addiction to wastefulness. This American habit, a "flagrant" aspect of American life (according to Ray Allen Billington), goes back to the settlement of the frontier.

> Why protect trees in a land where they grew by billions? Why preserve soil when a move to virgin fields was cheaper than fertilizer? . . . So the frontiersman felled forests, mined the soil with his wasteful farming methods, slaughtered game, honeycombed mountains with his mining shafts, overcropped pasturage with his herds, drained lakes, and altered the landscape as he moved in quest of wealth.[33]

In fairness there is, or was, a humane or even humanitarian side of America's wastefulness. Frontiersmen wanted to save themselves and their families body blows at the hands of nature, elements, and hard labor. They sacrificed resources and materials in order to spare their humanity. Later, during wartime, Americans would fight with a supersurfeit of military hardware in order to save American lives. Some still argue that it was the prodigious outpouring of American arms that turned the tide of World War II against the Nazis. In our own day this humane motive for waste is less convincingly seen in our prepared frozen foods ("pay more, suffer less") and in our throwaway domestic scene, which, with its "paper handkerchiefs and paper plates, metal cans, plastic containers, and no-deposit-no-return bottles," Billington judges a dubious heritage of the frontier.[34]

The national ethic of waste, once a way of cushioning the human and of celebrating abundance, is now far more a threat to our humanity than a benefit to it. It is a part of our American myth come to be destructive. It is now, in fact, a murderous luxury. For with every bite of excess protein, we Americans (and those in other developed nations) take food out of the mouths of hungry people in poor lands. We violate what has become a "nutritional system applicable to Mankind as a whole."[35]

3. Metaphors

How may we move to a better sense of identity and direction and to a better myth of the good life? We live in a sense by our metaphors, by the images we choose in order to conjure up whatever it is that we value, believe, want, or hope for. Americans long expressed their identity in metaphors of the frontier and the movement west: we were a nation of adventurers, settlers, cowboys. With the advent of the Machine Age, we became a nation on wheels: if we were going somewhere it was metaphorically (as well as literally) in an automobile.

Ecologists have seized on the metaphor of the lifeboat to warn us of the crisis we are in, and to jar us out of the easy metaphors to which we were accustomed in the past. Without denying the need for change, I must now ask whether the metaphor of the lifeboat is the best one for Americans to affirm just now as the shape of their new destiny.

I have already expressed various objections to the ethics of the lifeboat. It is chiliastic, it is of dubious morality, and it fixes responsibility at the wrong point, allowing the chief culprits —ourselves, the over-consumers and wasters of America and the West—to escape blame.

Now I must add a final objection. As a metaphor, lifeboat ethics encourages the worst mythical tendencies in our minds. The ethics of the lifeboat reinforces the temptation toward American neo-nationalism.

Self-absorption, says Garry Wills, has always been an American trait. America has been worse than isolationist much of the time: it has been solipsistic. The Vietnam tragedy should have taught us better, but it didn't.[36] Still to be urged to think of ourselves first, still to be told in effect that we may even yet contemplate the possibility of American disregard of the rest of the world (for this is, in the end, regardless of intent, the vision which lifeboat ethics fosters in the minds of most people), is to invite us to nourish the same ills that have produced our present national crisis. What must now be permanently discarded are all illusions about American options *vis à vis* the balance of mankind—the pretension that America, in a fancied aseity, could act as arbiter of the fate of all. Lifeboat ethics becomes one more proposal for an American "final solution" to the world's problems, It suggests that only we and those like us—the consuming nations—deserve to live.

Some of the old American myths have become destructive and must now be abandoned. One is that America is powerful enough to do whatever it wishes. Another is revived in the relatively recent Kissinger doctrine that America may disaffiliate and reaffiliate with the rest of the world at will. A third is that we can save ourselves through consumption, progress, and growth.

We must search the pantries of our heritage in order to find a new way of visualizing America's relationship to the rest of the world, and to better articulate what it is about America that can extend hope to other nations. Hardin's metaphor of the lifeboat is the worst possible image for accomplishing this goal. The metaphor proposed by another scientist, however—not an American, but a man who, like Hardin, saw the point of developing an appropriate metaphor before moving to technical work—may well be what we now seek. Pierre Teilhard de Chardin, a French paleontologist, biologist, and Jesuit priest, put forward the metaphor of the *wheat sheaf* to characterize the present condition and prospective future of mankind.

Human evolution, argued Teilhard, unlike the evolution of other living creatures, has shown a remarkable tendency toward convergence. It is true that if we look around us we can see all sorts of separations, conflicts, and compartments—ethnic, political, and religious. Overriding these differences, however, we can detect a persistent movement toward inter-communication and reunion. Scientists, for example, can come together and talk and agree on criteria and findings despite differences of race, religion, and language. Mankind is emerging from a recent past of separateness into a new organic whole. Mankind is being "planetized" at last, and Teilhard was certain that this is for the good, for it moves man toward a new and fuller identity.[37]

In animal evolution the pattern is like that of a fan, or like the finches of a given archipelago, radiating island by island in their diverse anatomical characteristics. But in man, the way we interact is better described as a tendency toward closure: "Like the petals of a gigantic lotus at the end of the day, we have seen human petals of planetary dimensions slowly closing in upon themselves."[38]

The life of man is thus like a sheaf of wheat, for no strand of it "is wholly independent in its growth of its neighboring threads." We may best visualize our human condition, said Teilhard, if "we regard the human group, . . . as simply a normal sheaf of phyla in which, owing to the emergence of a powerful field of attraction, the fundamental divergent tendency of the evolutionary radiations is overcome by a stronger force inducing them to converge."[39]

Does this new metaphor signal the end of American distinctiveness? Not at all. Let us hope it does speed the demise of

American arrogance. But the strands do not disappear or melt. They remain strands, even if the orienting reality is that of the sheaf.

America, we may say, is now invited by the course of human events to take its place in this convergence. Every strand in the interdependent sheaf of mankind has its own identity, its own past, its own heritage. It will now find meaning within that distinctive evolution—which appeared to be divergent before —through its synthesis in the new reality of the intertwined human experience.

Here is the context, then, for a new American and Western "fundamental myth": we are nearest to becoming ourselves when we see that we are part of the reconverging sheaf of humanity.

In a truly reunited world, America would come into her own for the first time, for she could spend her psychic and mythic energies on being herself, relieved of the burdens of proving her prowess as "second-to-none" or of "sweating out" the anxieties of a famine-induced survival ordeal. All of the healthy American cornerstones—voluntary association, technical initiative and know-how, democratic experience—could literally be proffered as the stuff of "best hopes" to the world. And they would be accepted as such by the remainder of this afflicted planet—as gifts no longer suspect.

NOTES

1. Garrett Hardin, "Living on a Lifeboat," *Bioscience* (October, 1974) 566. The italics are his.
2. Garrett Hardin, *Exploring New Ethics for Survival: The Voyage of the Spaceship Beagle* (Baltimore: Penguin Books, 1972), p. 224.
3. Sidney E. Ahlstrom, *A Religious History of the American People* (New Haven: Yale University Press, 1972), p. 479.
4. Emma Rothschild, "How Doomed Are We?," *New York Review* (June 26, 1975) 31; Thomas Y. Canby, "Can the World Feed Its People?," *National Geographic* (July, 1975) 29; Hardin, *Exploring New Ethics*, p. 175.
5. Emma Rothschild, "How Doomed Are We?," 31.
6. Geoffrey Barraclough, "The Great World Crisis I," *New York Review* (January 23, 1975) 26; Emma Rothschild, "A Reporter at Large: Short Term, Long Term," *New Yorker* (May 26, 1975) 40.
7. *Newsweek* (February 17, 1975) 76.
8. Alan Berg, "The Trouble with Triage," *New York Times Magazine* (June 15, 1975) 26, 28, 31.
9. Thomas Robert Malthus, *Population: The First Essay* (Ann Arbor: University of Michigan, Ann Arbor Paperbacks, 1959), p. 120.

10. Alan Berg, op. cit., 35.
11. Ibid.
12. Emma Rothschild, "A Reporter at Large," 68.
13. Ibid.
14. Reinhold Niebuhr, *Essays in Applied Christianity*, ed. D. B. Robertson (New York: Meridian Living Age Books, 1959), p. 103.
15. Garrett Hardin, *Exploring New Ethics for Survival*, pp. 129-30.
16. Reinhold Niebuhr, op. cit., pp. 80–81.
17. Ibid., pp. 79, 83.
18. Emma Rothschild, "How Doomed Are We?," 33.
19. Garrett Hardin, *Exploring New Ethics for Survial*, vii.
20. Ibid., p. 129.
21. Ibid., pp. 253, 261.
22. Garrett Hardin, "Living on a Lifeboat," 561.
23. *New York Times Magazine* (January 5, 1975) 45.
24. Garrett Hardin, *Exploring New Ethics for Survival*, p. 205.
25. *Houston Post* (July 21, 1975).
26. Richard Barnett and Ronald Müller, "A Reporter at Large: Global Reach—I", *New Yorker* (Dec. 2, 1972) 62, 64.
27. Ibid., pp. 62, 64.
28. Ibid., p. 84.
29. Richard Barnett and Ronald Müller, "A Reporter at Large," 114; Frances Moore Lappé, "Fantasies of Famine," *Harper's*, (February, 1975) 54.
30. Richard Barnett and Ronald Müller, op. cit., 115.
31. Frances Moore Lappé, op. cit., 54, 52, 89.
32. Ibid., pp. 52–53.
33. Ray Allen Billington, *America's Frontier Heritage* (New York: Holt, Rinehart and Winston, 1966), p. 169.
34. Ibid., p. 168. Cf. the remark of Gore Vidal: "Americans have always been lousy soldiers. . . . We win the occasional war . . . through our superior production of lethal toys," *New York Review*, supplement on "The Meaning of Vietnam" (June 12, 1975) 24.
35. Pierre Teilhard de Chardin, *The Future of Man*, tr. Norman Denny (New York: Harper & Row Torchbooks, 1964), p. 167.
36. Garry Wills, *New York Review*, supplement on "The Meaning of Vietnam" (June 12, 1975) 24.
37. Pierre Teilhard de Chardin, op. cit., pp. 142, 167.
38. Ibid., p. 188.
39. Ibid., p. 166.

CARRYING CAPACITY AS AN
ETHICAL CONCEPT

GARRETT HARDIN

LIFEBOAT ETHICS is merely a special application of the logic of the commons.[1] The classic paradigm is that of a pasture held as common property by a community and governed by the following rules: first, each herdsman may pasture as many cattle as he wishes on the commons; and second, the gain from the growth of cattle accrues to the individual owners of the cattle. In an underpopulated world the system of the commons may do no harm and may even be the most economic way to manage things, since management costs are kept to a minimum. In an overpopulated (or overexploited) world a system of the commons leads to ruin, because each herdsman has more to gain individually by increasing the size of his herd than he has to lose as a single member of the community guilty of lowering the carrying capacity of the environment. Consequently he (with others) overloads the commons.

Even if an individual fully perceives the ultimate consequences of his actions he is most unlikely to act in any other way, for he cannot count on the restraint *his* conscience might dictate being matched by a similar restraint on the part of *all* the others. (Anything less than all is not enough.) Since mutual ruin is inevitable, it is quite proper to speak of the *tragedy* of the commons.

Mr. Hardin is Professor of Biology at the University of California, Santa Barbara. He has given special attention to population biology and human ecology. The author of several books—including a widely used biology textbook and *Exploring New Ethics for Survival*—he has been one of the principal provocateurs of current discussions of lifeboat ethics and triage in relation to world famine.

Tragedy is the price of freedom in the commons. Only by changing to some other system (socialism or private enterprise, for example) can ruin be averted. In other words, in a crowded world survival requires that some freedom be given up. (We have, however, a choice in the freedom to be sacrificed.) Survival is possible under several different politico-economic systems —but not under the system of the commons. When we understand this point, we reject the ideal of distributive justice stated by Karl Marx a century ago, "From each according to his ability, to each according to his needs."[2] This ideal might be defensible if "needs" were defined by the larger community rather than by the individual (or individual political unit) *and if "needs" were static.*[3] But in the past quarter-century, with the best will in the world, some humanitarians have been asserting that rich populations must supply the needs of poor populations even though the recipient populations increase without restraint. At the United Nations conference on population in Bucharest in 1973 spokesmen for the poor nations repeatedly said in effect: "We poor people have the right to reproduce as much as we want to; you in the rich world have the responsibility of keeping us alive."

Such a Marxian disjunction of rights and responsibilities inevitably tends toward tragic ruin for all. It is almost incredible that this position is supported by thoughtful persons, but it is. How does this come about? In part, I think, because language deceives us. When a disastrous loss of life threatens, people speak of a "crisis," implying that the threat is temporary. More subtle is the implication of quantitative stability built into the pronoun "they" and its relatives. Let me illustrate this point with quantified prototype statements based on two different points of view.

Crisis analysis: ""*These* poor people (1,000,000) are starving, because of a crisis (flood, drought, or the like). How can we refuse *them* (1,000,000)? Let us feed *them* (1,000,000). Once the crisis is past those who are still hungry are few (say 1,000) and there is no further need for our intervention."

Crunch analysis: "*Those* (1,000,000) who are hungry are reproducing. We send food to *them* (1,010,000). *Their* lives (1,020,000) are saved. But since the environment is still essentially the same, the next year *they* (1,030,000) ask for more food. We send it to *them* (1,045,000); and the next year *they* (1,068,000) ask for still more. Since the need has not gone away, it is a mistake to speak of a passing crisis: it is evidently a permanent crunch that this growing "they" face—a growing disaster, not a passing state of affairs."

"They" increases in size. Rhetoric makes no allowance for a ballooning pronoun. Thus we can easily be deceived by language. We cannot deal adequately with ethical questions if we ignore quantitative matters. This attitude has been rejected by James Sellers, who dismisses prophets of doom from Malthus[4] to Meadows[5] as "chiliasts." Chiliasts (or millenialists, to use the Latin-derived equivalent of the Greek term) predict a catastrophic end of things a thousand years from some reference point. The classic example is the prediction of Judgment Day in the year 1000 anno Domini. Those who predicted it were wrong, of course; but the fact that this specific prediction was wrong is no valid criticism of the use of numbers in thinking. Millenialism is numerology, not science.

In science, most of the time, it is not so much exact numbers that are important as it is the relative size of numbers and the direction of change in the magnitude of them. Much productive analysis is accomplished with only the crude quantitation of "order of magnitude" thinking. First and second derivatives are often calculated with no finer aim than to find out if they are positive or negative. Survival can hinge on the crude issue of the sign of change, regardless of number. This is a far cry from the spurious precision of numerology. Unfortunately the chasm between the "two cultures," as C. P. Snow called them,[6] keeps many in the non-scientific culture from understanding the significance of the quantitative approach. One is tempted to wonder also whether an additional impediment to understanding may not be the mortal sin called Pride, which some theologians regard as the mother of all sins.

Returning to Marx, it is obvious that the *each* in "to each according to his needs" is not—despite the grammar—a unitary, stable entity: "each" is a place-holder for a ballooning variable. Before we commit ourselves to saving the life of *each* and every person in need we had better ask this question: "*And then what?*" That is, what about tomorrow, what about posterity? As Hans Jonas has pointed out,[7] traditional ethics has almost entirely ignored the claims of posterity. In an overpopulated world humanity cannot long endure under a regime governed by posterity-blind ethics. It is the essence of ecological ethics that it pays attention to posterity.

Since "helping" starving people requires that we who are rich give up some of our wealth, any refusal to do so is almost sure to be attributed to selfishness. Selfishness there may be, but focusing on selfishness is likely to be non-productive. In truth, a selfish motive can be found in all policy proposals. The selfishness of *not* giving is obvious and need not be elaborated. But the selfishness of giving is no less real, though more subtle.[8] Consider the sources of support for Public Law 480, the act of Congress under which surplus foods were given to poor countries, or sold to them at bargain prices ("concessionary terms" is the euphemism). Why did we give food away? Conventional wisdom says it was because we momentarily transcended our normal selfishness. Is that the whole story?

It is not. The "we" of the above sentence needs to be subdivided. The farmers who grew the grain did not give it away. They sold it to the government (which then gave it away). Farmers received selfish benefits in two ways: the direct sale of grain, and the economic support to farm prices given by this governmental purchase in an otherwise free market. The operation of P. L. 480 during the past quarter-century brought American farmers to a level of prosperity never known before.

Who else benefited —in a selfish way? The stockholders and employees of the railroads that moved grain to seaports benefited. So also did freight-boat operators (U. S. "bottoms" were specified by law). So also did grain elevator operators. So also did agricultural research scientists who were financially supported in a burgeoning but futile effort "to feed a hungry world."[9] And so also did the large bureaucracy required to keep the P. L. 480 system working. In toto, probably several million people personally benefited from the P. L. 480 program. Their labors cannot be called wholly selfless.

Who *did* make a sacrifice for P. L. 480? The citizens generally, nearly two hundred million of them, paying directly or indirectly through taxes. But each of these many millions lost only a little: whereas each of the million or so gainers gained a great deal. The blunt truth is that *philanthropy pays*—if you are hired as a philanthropist. Those on the gaining side of P.L. 480 made a great deal of money and could afford to spend lavishly to persuade Congress to continue the program. Those on the sacrificing side sacrificed only a little bit per capita and could not afford to spend much protecting their pocketbooks against philanthropic inroads. And so P. L. 480 continued, year after year.

Should we condemn philanthropy when we discover that some of its roots are selfish? I think not, otherwise probably no philanthropy would be possible. The secret of practical success in large-scale public philanthropy is this: see to it that the losses are widely distributed so that the per capita loss is small, but concentrate the gains in a relatively few people so that these few will have the economic power needed to pressure the legislature into supporting the program.

I have spent some time on this issue because I would like to dispose once and for all of condemnatory arguments based on "selfishness." As a matter of principle we should always assume that selfishness is *part* of the motivation of every action. But what of it? If Smith proposes a certain public policy, it is far more important to know whether the policy will do public harm or public good than it is to know whether Smith's motives are selfish or selfless. Consequences ("ends") can be more objectively determined than motivations ("means"). Situational ethics wisely uses consequences as the measure of morality. "If the end does not justify the means, what does?" asks Joseph Fletcher.[10] The obsession of older ethical systems with means and motives is no doubt in part a consequence of envy, which has a thousand disguises.[11] (Though I am sure this is true, the situationist should not dwell on envy very long, for it is after all only a motive, and as such not directly verifiable. In any case public policy must be primarily concerned with consequences.)

Even judging an act by its consequences is not easy. We are limited by the basic theorem of ecology, "We can never do merely one thing."[12] The fact that an act has many consequences is all the more reason for de-emphasizing motives as we carry out our ethical analyses. Motives by definition apply only to intended consequences. The multitudinous unintended ones are commonly denigrated by the term "side-effects." But "The road to hell is paved with good intentions," so let's have done with motivational evaluations of public policy.

Even after we have agreed to eschew motivational analysis, foreign aid is a tough nut to crack. The literature is large and contradictory, but it all points to the inescapable conclusion that a quarter of a century of earnest effort has not conquered world poverty. To many observers the threat of future disasters is more convincing now than it was a quarter of a century ago —and the disasters are not all in the future either.[13] Where have we gone wrong in foreign aid?

We wanted to do good, of course. The question, "How can we help a poor country?" seems like a simple question, one that should have a simple answer. Our failure to answer it suggests that the question is not as simple as we thought. The variety of contradictory answers offered is disheartening.

How can we find our way through this thicket? I suggest we take a cue from a mathematician. The great algebraist Karl Jacobi (1804–1851) had a simple stratagem that he recommended to students who found themselves butting their heads against a stone wall. *Umkehren, immer umkehren*—"Invert, always invert." Don't just keep asking the same old question over and over: turn it upside down and ask the opposite question. The answer you get then may not be the one you want, but it may throw useful light on the question you started with.

Let's try a Jacobian inversion of the food/population problem. To sharpen the issue, let us take a particular example, say India. The question we want to answer is, "How can we help India?" But since that approach has repeatedly thrust us against a stone wall, let's pose the Jacobian invert, "How can we *harm* India?" After we've answered this perverse question we will return to the original (and proper) one.

As a matter of method, let us grant ourselves the most malevolent of motives: let us ask, "How can we harm India—*really* harm her?" Of course we might plaster the country with thermonuclear bombs, speedily wiping out most of the 600 million people. But, to the truly malevolent mind, that's not much fun: a dead man is beyond harming. Bacterial warfare could be a bit "better," but not much. No: we want something that will really make India suffer, not merely for a day or a week, but on and on and on. How can we achieve this inhumane goal?

Quite simply: by sending India a bounty of food, year after year. The United States exports about 80 million tons of grain a year. Most of it we sell: the foreign exchange it yields we use for such needed imports as petroleum (38 percent of our oil consumption in 1974), iron ore, bauxite, chromium, tin, etc. But in the pursuit of our malevolent goal let us "unselfishly" tighten our belts, make sacrifices, and do without that foreign exchange.

Let us *give* all 80 million tons of grain to the Indians each year.

On a purely vegetable diet it takes about 400 pounds of grain to keep one person alive and healthy for a year. The 600 million Indians need 120 million tons per year; since their nutrition is less than adequate presumably they are getting a bit less than that now. So the 80 million tons we give them will almost double India's per capita supply of food. With a surplus, Indians can afford to vary their diet by growing some less efficient crops; they can also convert some of the grain into meat (pork and chickens for the Hindus, beef and chickens for the Moslems). The entire nation can then be supplied not only with plenty of calories, but also with an adequate supply of high quality protein. The people's eyes will sparkle, their steps will become more elastic; and they will be capable of more work. "Fatalism" will no doubt diminish. (Much so-called fatalism is merely a consequence of malnutrition.) Indians may even become a bit overweight, though they will still be getting only two-thirds as much food as the average inhabitant of a rich country. Surely—we think—surely a well-fed India would be better off?

Not so: *ceteris paribus*, they will ultimately be worse off. Remember, "We can never do merely one thing." A generous gift of food would have not only nutritional consequences: it would also have political and economic consequences. The difficulty of distributing free food to a poor people is well known. Harbor, storage, and transport inadequacies result in great losses of grain to rats and fungi. Political corruption diverts food from those who need it most to those who are more powerful. More abundant supplies depress free market prices and discourage native farmers from growing food in subsequent years. Research into better ways of agriculture is also discouraged. Why look for better ways to grow food when there is food enough already?

There are replies, of sorts, to all the above points. It may be maintained that all these evils are only temporary ones: in time, organizational sense will be brought into the distributional system and the government will crack down on corruption. Realizing the desirability of producing more food, for export if nothing else, a wise government will subsidize agricultural research in spite of an apparent surplus. Experience does not give much support to this optimistic view, but let us grant the conclusions for the sake of getting on to more important matters. Worse is to come.

The Indian unemployment rate is commonly reckoned at 30 percent, but it is acknowledged that this is a minimum figure. *Under*employment is rife. Check into a hotel in Calcutta with four small bags and four bearers will carry your luggage to the room—with another man to carry the key. Custom, and a knowledge of what the traffic will bear, decree this practice. In addition malnutrition justifies it in part. Adequately fed, half as many men would suffice. So one of the early consequences of achieving a higher level of nutrition in the Indian population would be to increase the number of unemployed.

India needs many things that food will not buy. Food will not diminish the unemployment rate (quite the contrary); nor will it increase the supply of minerals, bicycles, clothes, automobiles, gasoline, schools, books, movies, or televison. All these things require energy for their manufacture and maintenance.

Of course, food is a form of energy, but it is convertible to other forms only with great loss; so we are practically justified in considering energy and food as mutually exclusive goods. On this basis the most striking difference between poor and rich countries is not in the food they eat but in the energy they use. On a per capita basis rich countries use about three times as much of the primary foods—grain and the like—as do poor countries. (To a large extent this is because the rich convert much of the grain to more "wasteful" animal meat.) But when it comes to energy, rich countries use ten times as much per capita. (Near the extremes Americans use 60 times as much per person as Indians.) By reasonable standards much of this energy may be wasted (e.g., in the manufacture of "exercycles" for sweating the fat off people who have eaten too much), but a large share of this energy supplies the goods we regard as civilized: effortless transportation, some luxury foods, a variety of sports, clean space-heating, more than adequate clothing, and energy-consuming arts—music, visual arts, electronic auxiliaries, etc. Merely giving food to a people does almost nothing to satisfy the appetite for any of these other goods.

But a well-nourished people is better fitted to try to wrest more energy from its environment. The question then is this: Is the native environment able to furnish more energy? And at what cost?

In India energy is already being gotten from the environment at a fearful cost. In the past two centuries millions of acres of India have been deforested in the struggle for fuel, with the usual environmental degradation. The Vale of Kashmir, once one of the garden spots of the world, has been denuded to such an extent that the hills no longer hold water as they once did, and the springs supplying the famous gardens are drying up. So desperate is the need for charcoal for fuel that the Kashmiri now make it out of tree leaves. This wasteful practice denies the soil of needed organic mulch.

Throughout India, as is well known, cow dung is burned to cook food. The minerals of the dung are not thereby lost, but the ability of dung to improve soil tilth is. Some of the nitrogen in the dung goes off into the air and does not return to Indian soil. Here we see a classic example of the "vicious circle": because Indians are poor they burn dung, depriving the soil of nitrogen and making themselves still poorer the following year. If we give them plenty of food, as they cook this food with cow dung they will lower still more the ability of their land to produce food.

Let us look at another example of this counter-productive behavior. Twenty-five years ago western countries brought food and medicine to Nepal. In the summer of 1974 a disastrous flood struck Bangladesh, killing tens of thousands of people, by government admission. (True losses in that part of the world are always greater than admitted losses.) Was there any connection between feeding Nepal and flooding Bangladesh? Indeed there was, and is.[14]

Nepal nestles amongst the Himalayas. Much of its land is precipitous, and winters are cold. The Nepalese need fuel, which they get from trees. Because more Nepalese are being kept alive now, the demand for timber is escalating. As trees are cut down, the soil under them is washed down the slopes into the rivers that run through India and Bangladesh. Once the absorptive capacity of forest soil is gone, floods rise faster and to higher maxima. The flood of 1974 covered two-thirds of Bangladesh, twice the area of "normal" floods—which themselves are the consequence of deforestation in preceding centuries.

By bringing food and medicine to Nepal we intended only to save lives. But we can never do merely one thing, and the Nepalese lives we saved created a Nepalese energy-famine. The lives we saved from starvation in Nepal a quarter of a century ago were paid for in our time by lives lost to flooding and its attendant evils in Bangladesh. The saying, "Man does not live by bread alone," takes on new meaning.

Still we have not described what may be the worst consequence of a food-only policy: revolution and civil disorder. Many kind-hearted people who support food aid programs solicit the cooperation of "hard-nosed" doubters by arguing that good nutrition is needed for world peace. Starving people will attack others, they say. Nothing could be further from the truth. The monumental studies of Ancel Keys and others have shown that starving people are completely selfish.[15] They are incapable of cooperating with others; and they are incapable of laying plans for tomorrow and carrying them out. Moreover, modern war is so expensive that even the richest countries can hardly afford it.

The thought that starving people can forcefully wrest subsistence from their richer brothers may appeal to our sense of justice, *but it just ain't so*. Starving people fight only among themselves, and that inefficiently.

So what would happen if we brought ample supplies of food to a population that was still poor in everything else? They would still be incapable of waging war at a distance, but their ability to fight among themselves would be vastly increased. With vigorous, well-nourished bodies and a keen sense of their impoverishment in other things, they would no doubt soon create massive disorder in their own land. Of course, they might create a strong and united country, but what is the probability of that? Remember how much trouble the thirteen colonies had in forming themselves into a United States. Then remember that India is divided by two major religions, many castes, fourteen major languages and a hundred dialects. A partial separation of peoples along religious lines in 1947, at the time of the formation of Pakistan and of independent India, cost untold millions of lives. The budding off of Bangladesh (formerly East Pakistan) from the rest of Pakistan in 1971 cost several million more. All these losses were achieved on a low level or nutrition. The possibilities of blood-letting in a population of 600 million well-nourished people of many languages and religions and no appreciable tradition of cooperation stagger the imagination. Philanthropists with any imagination at all should be stunned by the thought of 600 million well-fed Indians seeking to meet their energy needs from their own resources.

So the answer to our Jacobian question, "How can we harm India?" is clear: send food *only*. Escaping the Jacobian by re-inverting the question we now ask, "How can we *help* India?"

Immediately we see that we must *never* send food without a matching gift of non-food energy. But before we go careening off on an intoxicating new program we had better look at some more quantities.

On a per capita basis, India uses the energy equivalent of one barrel of oil per year; the U. S. uses sixty. The world average of all countries, rich and poor, is ten. If we want to bring India only up to the present world average, we would have to send India about 9 x 600 million bbls. of oil per year (or its equivalent in coal, timber, gas or whatever). That would be more than five billion barrels of oil equivalent. What is the chance that we will make such a gift?

Surely it is nearly zero. For scale, note that our total yearly petroleum use is seven billion barrels (of which we import three billion). Of course we use (and have) a great deal of coal too. But these figures should suffice to give a feeling of scale.

More important is the undoubted psychological fact that a fall in income tends to dry up the springs of philanthropy. Despite wide disagreements about the future of energy it is obvious that from now on, for at least the next twenty years and possibly for centuries, our per capita supply of energy is going to fall, year after year. The food we gave in the past was "surplus." By no accounting do we have an energy surplus. In fact, the perceived deficit is rising year by year.

India has about one-third as much land as the United States. She has about three times as much population. If her people-to-land ratio were the same as ours she would have only about seventy million people (instead of 600 million). With the forested and relatively unspoiled farmlands of four centuries ago, seventy million people was probably well within the carrying capacity of the land. Even in today's India, seventy million people could probably make it in comfort and dignity —provided they didn't increase!

To send food only to a country already populated beyond the carrying capacity of its land is to collaborate in the further destruction of the land and the further impoverishment of its people.

Food plus energy is a recommendable policy; but for a large population under today's conditions this policy is defensible only by the logic of the old saying, "If wishes were horses, beggars would ride." The fantastic amount of energy needed for such a program is simply not in view. (We have mentioned nothing of the equally monumental "infrastructure" of political, technological, and educational machinery needed to handle unfamiliar forms and quantities of energy in the poor countries. In a short span of time this infrastructure is as difficult to bring into being as is an abundant supply of energy.)

In summary, then, here are the major foreign-aid possibilities that tender minds are willing to entertain:

a. Food plus energy—a conceivable, but practically impossible program.

b. Food alone—a conceivable and possible program, but one which would destroy the recipient.

In the light of this analysis the question of triage[8] shrinks to negligable importance. If *any* gift of food to overpopulated countries does more harm than good, it is not necessary to decide which countries get the gift and which do not. For posterity's sake we should never send food to any population that is beyond the realistic carrying capacity of its land. The question of triage does not even arise.

Joseph Fletcher neatly summarized this point when he said, "We should give if it helps but not if it hurts." We would do well to memorize his aphorism, but we must be sure we understand the proper object of the verb, which is the recipient. Students of charity have long recognized that an important motive of the giver is to help himself, the giver.[16] Hindus give to secure a better life in the next incarnation; Moslems, to achieve a richer paradise at the end of this life; and Christians in a simpler day no doubt hoped to shorten their stay in purgatory by their generosity. Is there anyone who would say that contemporary charity is completely free of the self-serving element?

To deserve the name, charity surely must justify itself primarily, perhaps even solely, by the good it does the recipient, not only in the moment of giving but in the long run. That every act has multiple consequences was recognized by William L. Davison, who grouped the consequences of an act of charity into two value-classes, positive and negative.[17] True charity, he said,

> confers benefits, and it refrains from injuring. . . . Hence, charity may sometimes assume an austere and even apparently unsympathetic aspect toward its object. When that object's real good cannot be achieved without inflicting pain and suffering, charity does not shrink from the infliction. . . . Moreover, a sharp distinction must be

drawn between charity and ambiability or good nature—the latter of which is a weakness and may be detrimental to true charity, although it may also be turned to account in its service.

To the ecologically-minded student of ethics, most traditional ethics looks like mere amiability, focusing as it does on the manifest misery of the present generation to the neglect of the more subtle but equally real needs of a much larger posterity. It is amiability that feeds the Nepalese in one generation and drowns Bangladeshi in another. It is amiability that, contemplating the wretched multitudes of Indians asks, "How can we let them starve?" implying that we, and only we, have the power to end their suffering. Such an assumption surely springs from hubris.

Fifty years ago India and China were equally miserable, and their future prospects equally bleak. During the past generation we have given India "help" on a massive scale; China, because of political differences between her and us, has received no "help" from us and precious little from anybody else. Yet who is better off today? And whose future prospects look brighter? Even after generously discounting the reports of the first starry-eyed Americans to enter China in recent years, it is apparent that China's 900 million are physically better off than India's 600 million.

All that has come about without an iota of "help" from us.

Could it be that a country that is treated as a responsible agent does better in the long run than one that is treated as an irresponsible parasite which we must "save" repeatedly? Is it not possible that robust responsibility is a virtue among nations as it is among individuals? Can we tolerate a charity that destroys responsibility?

Admittedly, China did not reach her present position of relative prosperity without great suffering, great loss of life. Did millions die? Tens of millions? We don't know. If we had enjoyed cordial relations with the new China during the birth process no doubt we would, out of a rich store of amiability, have seen to it that China remained as irresponsible and miserable as India. Our day-to-day decisions, with their delayed devastation, would have been completely justified by our traditional, posterity-blind ethics which seems incapable of asking the crucial question, "*And then what?*"

Underlying most ethical thought at present is the assumption that human life is the *summum bonum*. Perhaps it is; but we need to inquire carefully into what we mean by "human life." Do we mean the life of each and every human being now living, all 4,000,000,000 of them? Is each presently existing human being to be kept alive (and breeding) regardless of the consequences for future human beings? So, apparently, say amiable, individualistic, present-oriented, future-blind Western ethicists.

An ecologically-oriented ethicist asks, "And then what?" and insists that the needs of posterity be given a weighting commensurate with those of the present generation. The economic prejudice that leads to a heavy discounting of the future must be balanced by a recognition that the population of posterity vastly exceeds the population of the living.[18] We know from experience that the environment can be irreversibly damaged and the carrying capacity of a land permanently lowered.[14] Even a little lowering multiplied by an almost limitless posterity should weigh heavily in the scales against the needs of those living, once our charity expands beyond the limits of simple amiability.

We can, of course, increase carrying capacity somewhat. But only hubris leads us to think that our ability to do so is without limit. Despite all our technological accomplishments—and they are many—there is a potent germ of truth in the saying of Horace (65–8 B.C.): *Naturam expelles furca, tamen usque recurret.* "Drive nature off with a pitchfork, nevertheless she will return with a rush." This is the message of Rachel Carson,[19] which has been corroborated by many others.[20]

The morality of an act is a function of the state of the system at the time the act is performed—this is the foundation stone of situationist, ecological ethics.[12] A time-blind absolute ethical principle like that implied by the shibboleth, "the sanctity of life," leads to greater suffering than its situationist, ecological alternative —and ultimately and paradoxically, even to a lesser quantity of life over a sufficiently long period of time. The interests of posterity can be brought into the reckoning of ethics if we abandon the idea of the sanctity of (present) life as an absolute ethical ideal, replacing it with the idea of the sanctity of the carrying capacity.

Those who would like to make the theory of ethics wholly rational must look with suspicion on any statement that includes the word "sanctity." There is a whole class of terms whose principal (and perhaps sole) purpose seems to be to set a stop to inquiry: "self-evident" and "sanctity" are members of this class. I must, therefore, show that "sanctity" is used as something more than a discussion-stopper when it occurs in the phrase "the sanctity of the carrying capacity."

Some there are who so love the world of Nature (that is, Nature *sine* Man) that they regard the preservation of a world without humankind as a legitimate objective of human beings. It is difficult to argue this ideal dispassionately and productively. Let me only say that I am not one of this class of nature-lovers; my view is definitely homocentric. Even so I argue that we would do well to accept "Thou shalt not exceed the carrying capacity of any environment" as a legitimate member of a new Decalogue. When for the sake of momentary gain by human beings the carrying capacity is transgressed, the long-term interests of the same human beings—"same" meaning themselves and their successors in time—are damaged. I should not say that the carrying capacity is something that is *intrinsically* sacred (whatever *that* may mean) but that the rhetorical device "carrying capacity" is a shorthand way of dealing time and posterity into the game. A mathematician would, I imagine, view "carrying capacity" as an algorithm, a substitute conceptual element with a different grammar from the elements it replaces. Algorithmic substitutions are made to facilitate analysis; when they are well chosen, they introduce no appreciable errors. I think "carrying capacity" meets significant analytical demands of a posterity-oriented ethics.

In an uncrowded world there may be no ethical need for the ecological concept of the carrying capacity. But ours is a crowded world. We need this concept if we are to minimize human suffering in the long run (and not such a very long run at that). How Western man has pretty well succeeded in locking himself into a suicidal course of action by developing and clinging to a concept of the absolute sanctity of life is a topic that calls for deep inquiry. Lacking the certain knowledge that might come out of such a scholarly investigation, I close this essay with a personal view of the significance of—

CARRYING CAPACITY*

(To Paul Sears)

A man said to the universe:
"Sir, I exist!"
"However," replied the universe,
"The fact has not created in me
A sense of obligation."
              —Stephen Crane, 1899.

So spoke the poet, at century's end;
And in those dour days when schools displayed the world,
"Warts and all," to their reluctant learners,
These lines thrust through the layers of wishfulness,
Forming the minds that later found them to be true.

All that is past, now.
Original sin, then mere personal ego,
Open to the shafts of consciousness,
Now flourishes as an ego of the tribe
Whose battle cry (which none dare question) is
"Justice!"—But hear the poet's shade:

A tribe said to the universe,
"Sir, We exist!"
"So I see," said the universe,
"But your multitude creates in me
No feeling of obligation.

"Need creates right, you say? Your need, your right?
Have you forgot we're married?
Humanity and universe—Holy, indissoluble pair!
Nothing you can do escapes my vigilant response.

"Dam my rivers and I'll salt your crops;
Cut my trees and I'll flood your plains.
Kill 'pests' and, by God, you'll get a silent spring!
Go ahead—save every last baby's life!
I'll starve the lot of them later,
When they can savor to the full
The exquisite justice of truth's retribution.
Wrench from my earth those exponential powers
No wobbling Willie should e'er be trusted with:
Do this, and a million masks of envy shall create
A hell of blackmail and tribal wars
From which civilization will never recover.

*Copyright: Garrett Hardin, 1975.

"Don't speak to me of shortage. My world is vast
And has more than enough—for no more than enough.
There is a shortage of nothing, save will and wisdom;
But there is a longage of people.

"Hubris—that was the Greeks' word for what ails you.
Pride fueled the pyres of tragedy
Which died (some say) with Shakespeare.
O, incredible delusion! That potency should have no limits!
'We believe no evil 'til the evil's done'—
Witness the deserts' march across the earth,
Spawned and nourished by men who whine, 'Abnormal weather.'
Nearly as absurd as crying, 'Abnormal universe!' . . .
But I suppose you'll be saying that, next."

Ravish capacity: reap consequences.
Man claims the first a duty and calls what follows
Tragedy.
Insult—Backlash. Not even the universe can break
This primal link. Who, then, has the power
To put an end to tragedy? Only those who recognize
Hubris in themselves.

NOTES

1. Garrett Hardin, 1968: "The Tragedy of the Commons," *Science*, 162:1243–48.
2. Karl Marx, 1875: "Critique of the Gotha program." (Reprinted in *The Marx-Engels Reader*, Robert C. Tucker, editor. New York: Norton, 1972).
3. Garrett Hardin and John Baden (in press). *Managing the Commons*.
4. Thomas Robert Malthus, 1798: *An Essay on the Principle of Population, as it affects the Future Improvement of Society*. (Reprinted, *inter alia*, by the University of Michigan Press, 1959, and The Modern Library, 1960).
5. Donella H. Meadows, Dennis L. Meadows, Jorgen Randers, and William H. Behrens, 1972: *The Limits to Growth* (New York: Universe Books).
6. C. P. Snow, 1963: *The Two Cultures; and a Second Look* (New York: Mentor).
7. Hans Jonas, 1973: "Technology and Responsibility: Reflections on the New Task of Ethics," *Social Research*, 40:31–54.
8. William and Paul Paddock, 1967: *Famine–1975!* (Boston: Little, Brown & Co.).
9. Garrett Hardin, 1975: "Gregg's Law," *BioScience*, 25:415.
10. Joseph Fletcher, 1966: *Situation Ethics* (Philadelphia: Westminster Press).
11. Helmut Schoeck, 1969: *Envy* (New York: Harcourt, Brace & World).
12. Garrett Hardin, 1972: *Exploring New Ethics for Survival* (New York: Viking).
13. Nicholas Wade, 1974: "Sahelian Drought: No Victory for Western Aid," *Science*, 185:234–37.

14. Erik P. Eckholm, 1975: "The Deterioration of Mountain Environments," *Science*, 189:764–70.
15. Ancel Keys, et al., 1950: *The Biology of Human Starvation*. 2 vols. (Minneapolis: University of Minnesota Press).
16. A. S. Geden, 1928: "Hindu charity (almsgiving)," *Encyclopaedia of Religion and Ethics*, Vol. III, pp. 387–89 (New York: Scribner's).
17. William L. Davidson, 1928: "Charity," *Encyclopaedia of Religion and Ethics*, Vol. III, p. 373 (New York: Scribner's).
18. Garrett Hardin, 1974: "The Rational Foundation of Conservation," *North American Review*, 259 (4):14–17.
19. Rachel Carson, 1962: *Silent Spring* (Boston: Houghton Mifflin).
20. M. Taghi Farvar and John P. Milton, editors, 1969: *The Careless Technology*, (Garden City, N.Y.: Natural History Press).

RESPONSES

LIFEBOATERS AND MAINLANDERS:
A Response

DONALD W. SHRIVER, JR.

FOOD IS A BASIC HUMAN NECESSITY, and debate over food raises basic human questions. So the set of essays by Engelhardt, Fletcher, Hardin, Harrelson, Hinds, Lucas and Sellers will lead almost any reader to conclude. I have tried to summarize what appear to me to be the more important of these basic questions, raised either implicitly or explicitly by the essayists as a group. My own perspective in identifying the questions is that of a Christian ethicist. Other perspectives, like different lenses, might well lead one to pick out a different set of issues; but none of them belongs exclusively to a single discipline. That is an index to how basic they are.

1. What is the chief end of humanity?

The old Calvinist-catechetical question about the "chief end of man" had a crisp, single-minded answer: "to glorify God and to enjoy him forever." Monotheistic theologies are committed to some version of that singularity—some statement about the "ultimate meaning of existence." But assertions of ultimate meaning do not necessarily imply the dominance of a singular human value in human affairs. Values do not have to be arranged as a hierarchy; they might be conceived as clusters. A choice between

Mr. Shriver is President of the Faculty and William E. Dodge Professor of Applied Christianity at Union Theological Seminary in New York City. In his most recent book, *Spindles and Spires: A Re-Study of Religion and Social Change in Gastonia* (John Knox Press, 1976), he shares authorship with John Earle and Dean D. Knudson.

two such images of value relations seems called for, especially as one reads Joseph Fletcher and Walter Harrelson. Fletcher is willing to opt for "the tyranny of survival" (54), while Harrelson as willingly fits Fletcher's description of "idealists" who "have even been known to say they would rather die than go on living in a world where decisions to survive are made at the price of millions of lives" (53). Elsewhere Fletcher has stated that he is "quite certain that the great majority of people would, if need be, choose survival even at the expense of isolation and loneliness."[1] He could produce some formidable empirical evidence for his certainty. (The degradation of the Ik tribe in Uganda would do for a start.) But Harrelson could produce some equally compelling evidence, especially if the criterion of the compelling comes from the Bible—as it does for Harrelson. Certainly the New Testament does not advise Christians to consider their own physical lives as the "summum bonum." In the life of Jesus the temptation so to believe and so to act originated, we are told, in the *Devil.* The reply to the temptation (to turn stones into bread) was: "Man cannot live by bread alone."[2] I take this assertion to be accurate empirically as well as normatively: human life, reduced to a competitive scramble for bread, is already dehumanized life. Human life, as Bonhoeffer commented in his *Letters,* is meant to be lived "in many dimensions." The Biblical evidence implies as much—from the Garden of Eden to the eschatology of Jeremiah, from the multifold ministry of Jesus to the concern of an imprisoned Paul for books and clothes. Must we choose between food and music?

At the level of his theory of values, Garret Hardin should be first to concur with this distinction. "Hardin's law" says that "we can never do merely one thing" (124), because every act has diverse and diversely valuable consequences. Norman Faramelli has proposed an extension of Hardin's law to a second principle: "One solution by itself is inadequate."[3] Borrowing leaves from Geoffrey Vickers[4] and H. Richard Niebuhr,[5] I would propose a similar maxim: *One value by itself is inadequate.* The name of this theory is *pluralism,* and its explicit proponents in these pages are James Sellers and H. T. Engelhardt. "We should beware of any ethic that isolates and enthrones one value," says Sellers (110). Engelhardt sounds the same note by calling for a *multiplicity* of *mutual* obligations between food-giving and food-receiving countries of the world (75, 78). Rich societies may affirm the values of both comfort and beneficence while poor societies may prefer both progeny and asceticism. But optimized tradeoffs of values and benefits are conceivable within and between two such societies, each demanding some concession from the other while respecting the rights of the other to affirm its own value-priorities. Indians do have the right to have twice the children of Americans if they agree to tax the ecosystem half as much. In this sense, especially in negotiations between societies, there are no "absolute" values, but only complexes of value-preferences and value-relations. The point here is simply that on virtually *every* level of human existence—from the individual to the global interface of humanity and its environment—values are plural. Even the *bare* human necessities are *multiple*.

2. *Who should be the candidates for "benign neglect"?*

Like Engelhardt's desert isle, the lifeboat image reduces the elements of the ethical situation to a logically manageable image. But such images also focus the study of normative questions upon abnormal circumstances; and a good case can be made for the reverse order of logic: for grounding the analysis of "emergency ethics" in the "ethics of everyday." Not to do so is to run the danger of one form of Whitehead's fallacy of misplaced concreteness. Recent literature on ethics is full of questions like: If a good German finds himself ordered by the Nazi commander of the concentration camp to dispatch half the Jewish children to the ovens and half to the work camp, on what principles shall he choose between children? While not utterly insignificant, the question is far *less* significant than other questions about the social system that produced the question. At stake here is the *agenda-priority* of the empirical and moral analysis of lifeboat, battlefield, and famine situations. The *first* priority for such analysis concerns the prevention of shipwrecks, wars, and food shortfalls; the *second* priority, cutting the losses in such tragedies to a minimum; and *third*, which class of persons should be required to bear the heaviest loss.

Much of the triage literature slides easily into the implication that everything possible has now been done to attend to the first and the second priorities, so that the time for reckoning with the third has arrived. The dispute over this claim ripples through many of these essays. Collectively the authors do not agree on the amount of time and resources we still have to commit to the first two priorities. In this context James Sellers and Stuart Hinds are wise to call all the discussants to pay careful attention to their choice of metaphors and other language for *describing* the contemporary hunger problem. Are we, or are we not, already in the lifeboat and the battlefield situation in regard to hunger? Or is the time of those metaphors not yet? Let us be sure that the time has come for asking questions that should only be asked in emergencies!

Suppose, however, that the triagist is right: We are on the battlefield of famine. Who are the candidates whom "we" assign to death? (I put the pronoun in quotes because the identity of the decision-maker here is also a great issue in this whole debate.) Without assaying to state my own answer to this tragic question, I must merely observe that, on grounds of the triage-principle itself, the addiction of Hardin and Fletcher to classifying the write-offs by *nation* seems curious indeed. As Hinds makes clear, the principle was originally devised to distinguish between needy *individuals*. Classic liberal political philosophy would imply just that application. Classic socialism would decree an application to economic *classes*. Either alternative unit is as reasonable as the nation. Either would call for internal national discriminations between those who deserve and those who do not deserve food aid. On liberal grounds, welfare mothers with seven children prove themselves unfit for survival. On socialist grounds, greedy capitalist classes prove themselves unfit for survival—a claim that several writers here voice on behalf of Third World critics who are serious in their claim that "the world cannot afford another United States."

The captivity of the triage-moralists to the principle that Sellers calls "American neo-nationalism" (116) is unexamined in their argument. Some social unit must doubtless be chosen —dogmatically—as the proper object of applying the principle; but triagists seem hesitant to question the nation as the inevitable choice. Before they lift the knife of survivalist justice to the necks of whole nations, they should ask themselves about other ways that knife can cut—within their own countries, home towns, and families. As a specie of moral philosophy, the knife can as easily exclude welfare chiselers and Prodigal Sons galore from access to the pantry.

3. Who should produce more, and who should consume less?

Given his focus on the carrying capacity of global ecological systems, Garrett Hardin's nationalism seems especially curious. Why not treat the human element globally in that global system? The idea of mutual responsibility of two societies for not violating their own or each other's ecological limits, stressed by several of the triage-sympathizers, suggests that every part of the human system has potential obligations to every other part. Absolutistic notions of private property must fall before such a concept, of course, as before the classic Hebrew-Christian concept of stewardship. One would think that only a gross, survival-of-the-fittest evolutionist would disagree with George Lucas' view that "there is something inherently fraudulent about affluent peoples engaging in smug condemnation of the world's poor while seated at an overflowing supper table" (20). Food aid to the contrary, many current economic analyses have demonstrated that a net transfer of wealth is still going on from the poor to the rich countries. The fact that the rich *pay* for the transfer only proves that they are rich! "We tend to think of the poor world as heavily dependent on the rich for imports of food for survival," Frances Lappé reminds us. "In the poor world as a whole, however, only seven per cent of domestic consumption is supplied by imports. The rich countries are the major food importers"[6]—as the grain deals with Russia vividly demonstrate.

The disagreement here is clear, unmistakable, and momentous: By exempting affluent populations from accusations of resource-depletion, by awarding them the evolutionary badge of success, and by according them the right to ignore their own "population problem," triagists set themselves up for a counterblast of rage from Third Worlders fortified with *their* sense of ecological responsibility. At issue here, really, is the question of whose standpoint is *normative* for identifying "the problem." When Hardin says that "every Indian life saved through medical or nutritional assistance from abroad diminishes the quality of life for those who remain,"[7] he lays himself open to a double-charge of patronizing: Who is he—or any American—to make the judgment about diminished quality of life? (Why not ask "those who remain"?) And why are we so deaf to the empirical plausibility of the counterclaim: "Every *American* sustained at the cost of sixty times the resources now required to sustain an

Indian, diminishes the long-range quality of Indian life?" The counterclaim has its own empirical difficulties, but it grows out of a perfectly valid viewpoint—the Indian's relation to the same global ecosystem. On the whole, I would have to agree with Professor Donald R. Geiger's retort to Hardin: "The lifeboat proposal looks like what one might well expect from a nation which is at the top of the heap."[8]

4. Which principle of justice?

The principle of justice gets short shrift in some of the triage-advocates. We live in an unjust world, says Hardin. We live in a world where ethical principles are worth only so much as their practical results, says Fletcher. But in fact the triagists have their own particular principle of justice which they regard as ecologically irrefutable: "You get back from the system only what you put into it." One could call this either contributive or retributive justice. The stress here is on the first half of the famous Marxian norm: "from each according to his ability" (and, in return, only so much as active ability commands). The Marxian maxim introduces a second, qualifying principle: " . . . and to each according to his need." Hardin rejects this principle as destructive of a society in which each person makes his own judgment about "need" (121). Yet, contradictorily, he asserts the theoretical ability of our own society to make judgments about the "need" of other societies to control their population and to adopt overall energy-development policies (131). Increasingly, in rich countries like the United States, we will find ourselves compelled to make socially-enforced judgments about just such needs—e.g., as we decide whether the need of our own poor for better housing shall take energy-priority over the need of the Pentagon for improved weaponry.

But on the level of substantive ethical theory, the issue is whether or not justice must be defined strictly as an equal exchange of resources between equally able agents; or whether a qualifying "bias towards the weak" is a second, necessary principle. Biblical scholars have tended to find just that bias in the ethics of the Old and the New Testaments. Some concession to that principle seems to occupy Fletcher in the latter part of his essay, where he calls for a degree of sacrifice by affluent societies to enable the poor societies to "develop out of poverty" (65-66).

He will not subsidize the prolongation of mutual death; but his policy-proposals are apparently not so harsh as the ones promoted by Hardin, who seems to waver between a policy of "trade-not-aid" and "comprehensive-aid-for-some."[9] Christians, at least, have much reason in their tradition to attend carefully to the theoretical question here: whether a human world, organized around the principle "you get only what you give," is a truly human world. The issue is also the center of a long debate—now a century old—over what version of evolutionary theory matches the facts and the values of human history. Did human beings organize their societies without a kind of bias towards the weak—e.g., the extraordinarily weak human infant, whose fitness for survival depends strictly on the willingness of a family or a tribe to care for him according to his need? And if that rule for human life worked on a small scale to insure the survival of the specie, are we required to promote the survival of the specie on a global scale by some different rule? It is just possible that, over the millennia, compassion has been a key to human survival.

5. What relation between human values and human politics?

The issue of what version of evolutionary theory we are to consider "scientific" has been given eloquent exploration by Loren Eiseley, who believes that only through social cooperation did physically weak *homo sapiens* manage to survive the teeth and claws of the earliest human environment. Further, says Eiseley, the human's one superlative endowment, a brain, was remarkable not only for its power to anticipate (e.g., to make scientific predictions) but also for its power to value (e.g., to originate to some extent new "realities"). In this context, most notably in his book *The Firmament of Time,* Eiseley puts the quietus on the concept "nature." In its place he substitutes what theology has often called "history"—the record of the constant interplay of what human beings accept from their environment and what they create as new environment handed to the next generation. To downgrade this interplay—to imprison the future in the facts of the present—is *scientism.* In one of his recent writings, Hardin seems to embrace this error when he admits that the lifeboat ethic is hard to accept, "but—it's like gravity. We may not like the law of gravity either. But once you know it's true, you don't sit down and cry about it. That's the way the world is."[10] Even his ally Fletcher knows better than to make this mistake: "To go directly from 'is' to 'ought' is ethical foolishness" (58). Equally foolish is the illusion that every "ought" that enters the human brain can be realized in the outer world; but the point is that *both* the "scientific" and the "ethical" orientation towards the future are afflicted with *iffy-ness*. What kind of scientist is Hardin that he can be so sure about the behavior of an entire Asian nation on the brink of extinction by starvation? Are there not several plausible, fearsome scenarios to be written about such a tragedy? What sort of nuclear blackmail might a few well-fed Indian politicians devise for the occasion, in concert, perhaps, with the opportunistic Chinese? On the promising side, George Lucas is more "realistic" when he observes that the attempt to control human fertility "commits us to an enterprise *never before attempted* in human history" (20). We do not know if the enterprise is hopeful or hopeless—and we shall never know until we try, as Hinds tried in Turkey, producing a result that apparently surprised him and the demographers (44).

The discussion here turns strictly and inexorably towards "imponderables"; for neither does humanity live by ponderables alone. How very impatient (and how very American) Hardin must be to lament the fact that "a quarter of a century of earnest effort has not conquered world poverty" (124–25). Why, if we could be *sure* that it could be conquered in the next *two hundred years*, some of us would right now work even harder on the problem! And thereby would we demonstrate a very human relation between beliefs and perceptions. Reinhold Niebuhr used to say that "impossible ideals" are relevant to human affairs because they stretch the boundaries of the currently possible to embrace new possibilities. Scientific predictions of the future are *ethically* useful to the extent that they permit the predictors both to respect the inertias of the present and to redirect some of them towards a different future.

In my opinion the ecologists and the triage-moralists have made a genuine contribution to contemporary consciousness by introducing us to the concept of responsible relations between present and future generations of humanity. They also make a good case for mutual, multiple relations of responsibility between members of the present generation living in different parts of a global environment with limited carrying capacity. The case for population controls as the reciprocal of development aid is especially convincing. But the downgrading of the notion of humanity as one body whose members have "the same care for one another,"[11] is unwarranted—at least from the Hebrew-Christian perspective. If they bring nothing else to the processes of global politics, religiously and ethically sensitive persons can surely bring this: a vision of history as the return of the lifeboats to the continent of humanity. If they settle for the lifeboat-image of the human future, they will add their weight to all the other forces in the world that tempt us all first to believe, and then with our actions to prove, that John Donne was wrong to claim "no man is an island." Sellers describes the moralist as one who, "given a dispute on the facts, . . . chooses those assumptions that support brotherhood. He is aware of the risk he runs" (106), including the risk of underselling the future. Moral people complement the if's of science with some if's of faith, hope, and charity. At minimum, they insist that on occasion even an unlikely future must be given all possible chance to become likely. "Unrestrained idealism"[12] may indeed be a threat to clear thinking about these matters; but so also is unrestrained realism. Ideals, said Max Weber, may not run the engine of history, but they may serve as critical "switching points" directing society down one or another alternate track into the future.[13] Some consequentialists may believe that science or some other authority can give us exact, sufficient information about the impact of the present upon the future. In the serenity of that faith, they can remain consistent consequentialists. But those of us who see our world more hospitable to risk and uncertainty, more regularly assaulted by the contingencies of history, want our predictions of consequence laced with a few rules which are no less, and no more, fallible than scientific predictions. Better an ethic that tells us "what to strive for" than one which tells us only what to settle for. As John Rawls puts it: "at some point the priority of rules for nonideal cases will fail . . . , but we must try to postpone the day of reckoning as long as possible, and try to arrange society so that it never comes."[14]

NOTES

1. In George R. Lucas, Jr., "Famine and Global Policy: An Interview with Joseph Fletcher," *The Christian Century* (September 3–10, 1975), 757.
2. Luke 4:4.

3. Norman J. Faramelli, "Life Boat Ethics: The Case for Genocide by Benign Neglect," *Church and Society* (March–April 1975), 43.

4. Cf. Vickers, *The Art of Judgment: A Study in Policy Making* (New York: Basic Books, 1965) and *Value Systems and Social Process* (London: Penguin Books, 1970), especially chapter 6 of the latter, "The Multi-Valued Choice."

5. Cf. Niebuhr's now-classic essay, "The Center of Value," in *Radical Monotheism and Western Culture* (New York: Harper and Brothers, 1960), pp. 100–13. Niebuhr's relational value theory steers a clear course between absolutism and relativism in a way that should command much interest from ecologists and theologians, as is suggested in this pair of quotations:

    . . . nothing is valuable in itself, but everything has value, positive and negative, in its relations (107).

    Dogma, doubtless, there must be, since the analysis of value cannot begin in the void but must start with an act of decision for some being as value-center. But the dogmatism of a relativism which assumes the privileged position of one finite reality, such as man, is so narrow that it cuts off inquiry into great realms of value, and tends to confine the discussion of the good to an arbitrarily chosen field, for instance to that of the human good (112).

6. Frances Lappé, "Fantasies of Famine," *Harper's* (February, 1975), 54.

7. Quoted in the "Letters" section of *BioScience*, 25 (3):146, from his article on "Lifeboat Ethics" in the previous issue of this journal, 24 (10):561–68.

8. Letter, Ibid.

9. In his "Author's Reply," Ibid., (p. 148), Hardin makes clear his distaste even for the triage-ethic, which, after all, is a guideline for aid-giving. He believes that international relations should work exclusively on the principle of trade, not aid—so that his flirtation with a "food plus energy" program in his essay here is only a flirtation. ". . . The practice of trade recognizes the ancient legal principle of *quid pro quo,* a principle surely founded in biology. Replacing trade by one-way transfers of wealth produces parasitism."

10. As quoted in Wade Greene, "Triage," *The New York Times Magazine* (January 5, 1975). On Eiseley's rejection of scientist versions of evolutionary theory, cf. his three books: *The Immense Journey* (New York: Random House, Inc., 1957), *The Firmament of Time* (New York: Atheneum, 1969), and *The Unexpected Universe* (New York: Harcourt, Brace, and World, Inc., 1969).

11. I Corinthians 12:25.

12. Fletcher's phrase in Lucas, op. cit., 756.

13. Cf. Max Weber, "The Social Psychology of the World Religions," in H. H. Gerth and C. Wright Mills, eds., *From Max Weber: Essays in Sociology* (New York: Oxford University Press, 1958), p. 280.

14. John Rawls, *A Theory of Justice* (Cambridge: Harvard University Press, 1971), pp. 289, 303.

MUDDLED METAPHORS:
An Asian Response to Garrett Hardin

PAUL VERGHESE

I AGREE WITH PROFESSOR HARDIN on one point. We can scarce-
ly think without metaphors. But I also believe that wrong
metaphors are a sure mark of muddled thinking. An analogy, of
course, can never be totally coincident with the reality that it is
intended to illuminate. But in some essential features at least it
must conform. Hardin contends that the widespread use of the
spaceship metaphor to describe the plight of our planet is inappropriate, except perhaps as a justification for certain pollution
control measures. He proposes the lifeboat metaphor as an
alternative.

That proposal, however, seems to me a rather clear case of
"advanced muddlement." If there is one conclusion that is growing upon most informed persons in our time, it is the idea that we
are all "in the same boat." Yet Hardin, with this proposed
metaphor, would force us back into the outdated and fallacious
world view of national sovereignty and of the autonomous existence of each nation. In fact no nation is an island or a lifeboat;
we all sink together or float together. Professor Hardin may
have talked with some recent Indian or East European immi-
grants who gave him the idea that all the world wants to come to
America. But how preposterous an idea! There may indeed be a
few naive people in India, for example, who think that the

Dr. Verghese (Metropolitan Paulos Gregorios) is Bishop of the Orthodox
Syrian Church of the East, and Principal of the Orthodox Theological Seminary (Kottayam) in Kerala, India. He has special interest in ecumenical theology and in international church and political policy. He has worked extensively
over the past several years in and through the World Council of Churches.

solution to the problems of their nation is for some Indians to migrate to the U.S.A., Canada, or Australia. But no responsible government official or writer in India would give expression to such a point of view.

I prefer Professor Hardin's earlier metaphor of "the commons." But in the present case "the commons" is the world, and some of the "sheep" which graze it are more voracious than others. American "sheep" are consuming annually some thirty times as much per capita as are African or Asian "sheep." The real danger to the commons comes from the former, who consume too much, elbow the others aside, and thus destroy the commons. If there is to be equitable population control, the American rate of growth should be about one-thirtieth of what it is in Asia and Africa. The only way to save the commons is to starve the "fat sheep" and stop them from multiplying at all! For that goal we require persons and governments with a sense of justice as fairness, in order to control the world commons.

Population control on a world-wide scale is indeed necessary and essential. But whence this idea that all the spare room is in the "rich lifeboats" and that all the poor ones are overcrowded? In fact, many countries in Africa are really underpopulated in terms of the potential "carrying capacity" of their regional environments. Hence a nation like Tanzania refuses to have much to do with population control measures. Indeed, some of the most overcrowded nations are in industrially-advanced Western Europe.

But population control is only part of the problem of world justice, a question which turns as much on the relationships *between* nations as it does on the relationships *within* individual nations. The lifeboat ethics approach beclouds both these aspects of world justice. The spaceship metaphor, by contrast, deals with five critical dimensions of the justice problem in one stroke—all five arising from the nature of the human impact on the planet we inhabit: a) population pressure, food scarcity, and the evils of urban agglomeration; (b) thoughtless and potentially catastrophic resource and energy utilization; (c) unrestrained consumerism and industrial development leading to pollution, loss of human values, and disruption of the eco-balance necessary for the continuation of life on this planet; (d) the foolish trends towards greater and greater defense spending involving colossal waste of resources and the threat of a nuclear holocaust;

and (e) the partial blindness that besets human perception, due to an unwarranted over-reliance on science and technology to uncover the dimensions of the cosmos.

None of these problems can be adequately tackled on the basis of a lifeboat metaphor, whereas the spaceship metaphor bids fair to be a suitable framework within which to incorporate all five aspects of the human impact on the environment. All five are international problems—not matters for individual nations to tinker with on their own in their separate "lifeboats."

SURVIVAL ETHICS AND GLOBAL JUSTICE

All the "fatal metaphors" currently summoned to our aid in analyzing the problem of world hunger have one end in common—survival. The trend in the advocacy of lifeboat ethics leaves little doubt about whose survival is being contemplated. Clearly, survival is intended for those who already happen to be on board a lifeboat in uncrowded numbers, with well-supplied larders, existing well within some determined "safety margin." This is the "third alternative" which Professor Hardin recommends in solution of the current distribution crisis. The first alternative—survival of the human race as a whole—is foolish to aim for. Complete justice leads only to complete catastrophe. Alternative two is to admit a few more persons to the well-supplied lifeboats. Yet it is difficult, Hardin argues, to find a criterion by which to choose those few; and making the choice sacrifices the small "safety factor" for survival. So why discriminate? Let the whole lot perish, so that the few may survive (vicariously, of course, for the sake of the others).

This is characteristic pragmatic reasoning, and Professor Hardin stands within this influential western tradition. He takes quite seriously the "pragmatic maxim" of C. S. Pierce (1878): "Consider what effects, that might conceivably have practical bearings, we conceive the object of our conception to have. Then our conception of these effects is the whole of our conception of the object." Truth can be judged only by its cash value. The general truth of the planet is the struggle for existence, and victory is to the strong and unprincipled. If nature is red in tooth and claw, then why shy away from apparent blood and cruelty, if that is finally necessary for survival?

Herbert Spencer already had made clear this important concept, which Windelband terms the *naturwissenschaftliche* way of thought. We understand reality in terms of the laws of nature, rather than through arbitrary questions of ideal value. Indeed, this form of "evolutionary ethics" was germinally present in Bentham's formulation of utilitarianism which, by the turn of the last century, had become the principal moral justification for egoism and self-interest.

The ethics we hear today in Garrett Hardin's lifeboat ethics is the ethics of nineteenth-century Imperialism, Capitalism and Individualism. It places survival as the higher value, and ignores the plea for justice as mere feeble groaning by the pusillanimous, the weak, and the condemned. It takes courage to ignore that groaning and to act decisively for survival. If one starts paying back to the poor of the world what heretofore has been taken from them (such as restoring to native Americans a portion of their lands and possessions), then one has begun to dig one's own grave. Indeed, charity corrupts the poor. As Dr. Hardin states—with the characteristic realism of the tough and the strongwilled, determined to survive—*"Every life saved this year in a poor country diminishes the quality of life for subsequent generations."*[1] This is merely a thinly-veiled form of nineteenth-century imperialist-capitalist language, all too familiar to those acquainted with its history. If an improved wage is given the laborer, he will merely waste it on alcohol; so keep him poor and indigent for his own good. This, too, is a familiar rationalization of the unjust industrialists' rapacious greed and selfishness. "Survival before justice"—that is the creed of capitalism. Hardin merely offers us a contemporary reformulation and forthright presentation of this still-unobsolete creed.

Garrett Hardin is interested in a world government which is "sovereign in reproductive matters," but apparently not in a one which ensures justice to all. The United States is not a self-sufficient lifeboat. It is heavily dependent upon the markets and raw materials of the rest of the world. No nation is a self-sufficient lifeboat. There are no lifeboats, and we are not on lifeboats. We are in a spaceship on collision course, a spaceship without captain or crew, a spaceship without any lifeboat on board. We survive or perish together. That is the matter of fact. "Lifeboat Ethics" is a fantasy based upon a false metaphor; the spaceship metaphor, with all necessary qualifications, is the best we now have.

It is finally a matter of judgment to claim that justice is a higher value than mere survival. This is a judgment which I personally find informed by a Christian moral consciousness. It is undignified for persons to cling to life in selfishness and ignore the demands of justice. That way is morally erroneous and prudentially unwise. He who seeks to save his own life will lose it. He who is prepared to lose it for the sake of others will gain it. This does not mean that one should be a fool in opening the doors of one's house to all comers or by distributing one's largesse among all and sundry. The debate is not about open immigration policy or about aid of the "P.L. 480" type. The debate is about justice—not perfect justice, but more justice than we now enjoy. Professor Hardin, in my opinion, distorts the issue and confuses our judgment by pretending that the world is merely begging for free immigration to America and for free food aid. The demand from this corner of the globe [Kerala, India], at least, is that all should be able to work and all should be able to live, and that we should regulate together the opportunities for all. In opposition to Hardin, the demand is that the rich nations cooperate with the poor nations in creating a world structure with justice, and in working toward a civilization less consumption-oriented, less polluting, less wasteful, less war-minded, and more cautious about conserving ecostability. This demand is made upon the collective will of humanity in order that we might bring our spaceship under conscious and rational control, and establish justice, equity and sanity on board.

CONCLUSION

Regardless of their many and diverse opinions, all participants in the present debate seem to agree on a few basic points. There is urgent pressure on humanity everywhere to perceive clearly and to act to address some problems which are so acute that they will, if left unresolved, lead to certain disaster. These problems uncover pressing needs for:

a) a federally related global agency for population control;
b) a federally organized international agency which controls and restrains resource and energy utilization on the planet;
c) a federally organized and responsible global agency with sufficient funds and authority for pollution control and for the regulation of industrial development;
d) a world authority for regulation of trade and commerce among the nations;
e) a world authority with power to enforce disarmament—general as well as nuclear.

In detail, all these matters are controversial and difficult to implement. But humankind must ever set its mind to these problems, and seek manageable interim solutions while yet keeping these five, long-term objectives in view. The temporary myopia fostered by the current aura of crisis and by the current employment of the fallacious lifeboat metaphor must not serve to dissuade us from these momentous tasks.

NOTES

1. "Living on a Lifeboat," *BioScience*, XX (October, 1974), 565. Italics by author.

SELECT BIBLIOGRAPHY

Barraclough, Geoffrey. "The Great World Crisis." *New York Review* (23 January 1975).

Behrman, Corsa & Freedman, eds. *Fertility And Family Planning: A World View* (Ann Arbor, Michigan: University of Michigan Press, 1970).

Berg, Alan. "Industry's Struggle with World Malnutrition." *Harvard Business Review* (January-February, 1972) 130-42.

_____."The Trouble with Triage." *New York Times Magazine* (15 June 1975).

Borgese, Elizabeth Mann. "The Blue Revolution: Harvesting the Fruits of the Sea." *Center Report* (April 1975) 18-19.

Brown, Lester R. *World Without Borders.* (New York: Vintage Press, 1973).

_____. *In The Human Interest* (New York: W.W. Norton & Co., 1974).

_____. and Eckholm, Erik P. *By Bread Alone* (New York: Praeger Publishers, 1974).

_____. "Next Steps Toward Global Food Security." in *The U.S. And World Development,* J.W. Howes, *et. al.,* eds. (New York: Praeger Publishers, 1975) 72-86.

Callahan, Daniel. "Doing Well by Doing Good." *Hastings Report IV* (6) December, 1974.

_____. *The Tyranny Of Survival.* (New York: Macmillan & Co., 1973).

_____. ed. *The American Population Debate* (New York: Anchor Books, 1971).

Canby, Thomas Y. "Can the World Feed its People?" *National Geographic* (July 1975).

de Castro, Josue. *The Geography Of Hunger* (Boston: Little, Brown & Co., 1952).

Eckholm, Erik P. "The Deterioration of Mountain Environments." *Science CLXXXIX* (1975): 764-70.

Ehrlich, Paul. *The Population Bomb.* rev. ed. (New York: Ballantine Books, 1971).

_____and Ehrlich, Anne. *Population, Resources, Environment: Issues in Human Ecology.* rev. ed. (San Francisco: W.H. Freeman & Co., 1972).

Faramelli, Norman J. "Lifeboat Ethics: The Case for Genocide by Benign Neglect."
       Church And Society (March-April, 1975) 36-44.

Farvar, M. Taghi, & Milton, John P. eds. *The Careless Technology* (Garden City,
       N.Y.: Natural History Press, 1969).

Fletcher, Joseph. "Triage and Lifeboat Ethics: Moral Evaluation of a Social Policy."
       in *Triage In Medicine And Society,* G.R. Lucas, Jr., ed. (Houston: Institute of
       Religion, 1975) 23-34.

_____. *Situation Ethics* (Philadelphia: Westminster Press, 1966).

Greeg, Alan. "A Medical Aspect of the Population Problem." *Science CXXI* (1955)
       681-82.

Greene, Wade. "Triage: Who Shall be Fed? Who Shall Starve?" *New York Times
       Magazine* (5 January 1975).

Hardin, Garrett. *Exploring New Ethics For Survival: The Voyage Of The Spaceship
       Beagle* (New York: Viking Press, 1972).

_____. "Gregg's Law." *Bioscience XXV* (7) July 1975; 415.

_____. "Another Face of Bioethics: The Case for Massive 'Diebacks' of Population."
       Modern Medicine LXV (1 March 1975).

_____. "Ten Charming Delusions about Population." *American Biology Teacher*
       (February 1975) 102-3.

_____. "Rights, Human and Nonhuman: The Rational Basis of Conservation."
       North American Review (Winter 1974) 14-17.

_____. "Living on a Lifeboat." *Bioscience XXIV* (10) October, 1974; 561-68.

_____. "Lifeboat Ethics: The Case Against Helping the Poor." *Psychology Today*
       (September, 1974).

_____. "Ecological Conservatism." *Chemical And Engineering News XLIX* (28)
       12 July 1971.

_____. "Nobody Ever Dies of Overpopulation." *Science CLXXI* (3971) 12 February
       1971; 527.

_____. "The Tragedy of the Commons." *Science CLXII* (13 December 1968) 1243-
       48.

_____. & Baden, John. *Managing The Commons,* in press.

Hewes, Laurence J., Jr. "U.S. Short Term Food Policy Alternatives." *Center Report*
       (April 1975) 7-9.

Hinds, Stuart W. "Triage in Medicine." in *Triage in Medicine and Society,* G.R.
       Lucas, Jr. ed. (Houston: Institute of Religion, 1975) 6-22.

Howe, James W. & Sewell, J.H. "Triage and Other Challenges to Helping Poor
       Countries Develop." in *The U.S. and World Development,* J.W. Howe, et. al.,
       eds. (New York: Praeger Publishers, 1975) 55-71.

Joas, Hans: "Technology and Responsibility: Reflections on the New Tasks of Ethics."
       Social Research XL (1973) 31-54.

Keyes, Ancel, et. al. *The Biology Of Human Starvation,* 2 vols. (Minneapolis: Univer-
       sity of Minnesota Press, 1950).

Lappe, Francis Moore. "Fantasies of Famine," *Harper's* (February 1975).

Lucas, George R. Jr. *Triage in Medicine and Society* (Houston: Institute of Religion,
       1975).

_____. "Famine and Global Policy: An Interview with Joseph Fletcher." *The Chris-
       tian Century XCII* (28) 3-10 September 1975; 753-58.

Malloy, Michael T. " 'Let 'Em Starve!' A New Approach to World Hunger." *The
       National Observer* (29 March 1975).

Malthus, Thomas Robert. *An Essay On The Principle Of Population* (London, 1798) reprinted *inter alia* (Ann Arbor, Michigan: University of Michigan Press, 1959); (Modern Library, 1960).

Paddock, Paul and William. *Famine—1975!* (Boston: Little, Brown & Co., 1967).

Revelle, Roger. "The Ghost at the Feast." *Science CLXXXVI* (4164) 15 November 1974.

Lord Ritchie-Calder. "Triage=Genocide." *Center Report* (June 1975).

Rothschild, Emma. "How Doomed Are We?" *New York Review* (26 June 1975).

Simon, Laurence. "The Ethics of Triage." *Christian Century* (1-8 January 1975) 12-16.

A Word About *SOUNDINGS*

Since it began publication in 1968 *Soundings* has attracted a growing readership through its imaginative explication of issues and topics which enhance and illumine the human enterprise. *Soundings'* preoccupation with themes of value, meaning, and purpose has always been coupled with scholarship of the first order. Indeed, this unique combination has become *Soundings'* trademark. As the Editor, Thomas W. Ogletree, says:

> *Soundings* is a scholarly journal which seeks to challenge the fragmentation of learning present in modern intellectual life. Experience with the limits of specialization has given rise to a hunger for a new kind of scholarship, one reflecting high levels of professional competence, but at the same time embodying a paramount interest in the values which dignify human life. *Soundings* wishes to encourage scholarship which uses the materials and methods of established disciplines to address scholars in all areas of human inquiry. Such efforts are then available for fruitful interdisciplinary dialogue on common human concerns.

To this end *Soundings* has published issues which have included articles by such authors as Michael Polanyi, Rosemary Ruether, Garrett Hardin, Robert Bellah, Michael Novak, James Gustafson, Richard Rubenstein, and William O. Douglas. Topics have ranged from literary criticism and the book of Job to

161

Rawls' theory of justice to John Brown and the psychology of antinomian violence to audience and form in contemporary American poetry.

Each year *Soundings* publishes a special issue which seeks to focus the insights of different disciplines on a topic of contemporary importance. Recently *Soundings* has published such issues on structuralism; literature and politics; leisure, retirement and aging; the rediscovery of ethnicity; family, communes and utopian societies.

Soundings subscription rates are $10 for one year, $17 for two, and $23 for three with student subscriptions at the reduced rate of $7 per year. *Soundings'* address is P.O. Box 6309, Station B, Nashville, Tennesse 37235.

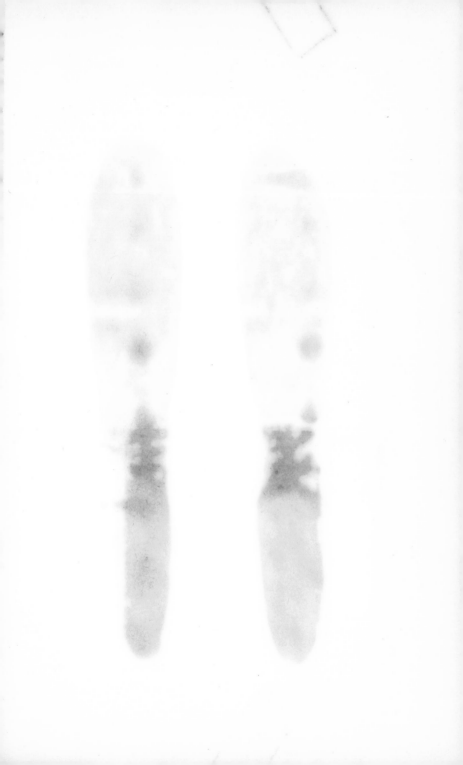

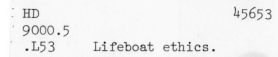